Let the Dog Decide

"Dale Stavroff a great trainer. His deceptively simple techniques are based on a true understanding of the psychology of dogs and the dog-human bond. Our dog, Lucy, is not only well behaved but is happy, confident and a delight to own. If you want to have a great relationship with your dog, the Stavroff method is just what you need."
—GIL CATES, multi-year producer of the "Academy Awards" broadcast, and Dr. Judith Reichman, author of *I'm Too Young to Get Old*

"Following Dale Stavroff's methods with my search and rescue dog has not only produced a happy, dedicated dog who is calm, patient, has a sense of self, and can solve problems, it has also helped me grow into a much better handler and trainer."
—GEORGIA COMBES, Secretary of the British Columbia Search Dog Association

"When I took my puppy to one of Dale Stavroff's seminars, he demonstrated in just a few minutes how quickly correct habits could be formed and a solid foundation for future training established. His teachings have opened doors to give everyday pet owners the chance to have a better relationship with their canine companions."
—LISA SHUPE, pet owner

"Dale Stavroff was recommended to me when I purchased my first German Shepherd, Buddy, to be my partner in search and rescue work. Not long after Buddy completed his training, he found four lost hunters in almost blizzard conditions. Whether you want a faithful family companion or a dedicated working dog, I highly recommend Dale Stavroff's unique training system."
—LINDA S. PHELPS, search and rescue worker

"Through all the training methods we had previously used, our beloved dog, K.D., had become aggressive, confused, and unhappy. Dale Stavroff taught us how to instill a desire in the dog to learn and a willingness to do the right thing. K.D. soon became an excellent partner and friend. If you are looking for the best way to give yourself and your dog a wonderful life together, you owe it to both of you to use Dale's gentle, positive methods."
—PAUL and PENNY SENOV, pet owners

"Thanks to Dale Stavroff's methods, my search and rescue dog responds instantly, joyfully and reliably to any behavioral cue and her search work is impeccable. I have also seen many dogs declared hopeless by other trainers, only to become well-behaved, enjoyable pets when they are trained Dale's way. In a lifetime of dog ownership, in which I have spent thousands of dollars and countless hours searching for the best training, I have never seen a trainer with more knowledge, understanding and skill in training dogs, and teaching their owners how to train, than Dale Stavroff."
—EILEEN PORTER, Klickitat County (Washington) Sheriff's Office Search and Rescue team

Dale Stavroff is a pioneer in positive motivational dog training that empowers both dogs and their owners. He has trained championship winning dogs of many breeds in conformation dog shows, obedience trials, and dog sports competitions. He trains dogs for search and rescue, explosives detection, and other service work, and he is a frequent lecturer on these and other training topics. He lives with his family in British Columbia. Visit him at www.precisiondogs.com.

Let the Dog Decide

The Revolutionary

15-Minute-a-Day

Program to Train Your Dog—

Gently and Reliably

Dale Stavroff

MARLOWE & COMPANY
NEW YORK

LET THE DOG DECIDE:
*The Revolutionary 15-Minute-a-Day Program
to Train Your Dog—Gently and Reliably*

Copyright © 2007 by Dale Stavroff
All interior photographs, with the exception of page iii, by Georgia
Combes. Photograph of author and Tiggie on page iii by Thian Wong.

Published by
Marlowe & Company
An Imprint of Avalon Publishing Group, Incorporated
245 West 17th Street • 11th Floor
New York, NY 10011-5300

AVALON
publishing group incorporated

Library of Congress Cataloging-in-Publication Data

Stavroff, Dale.
    Let the dog decide : the revolutionary 15-minute-a-day program to train
your dog gently and reliably / Dale Stavroff.
        p. cm.
    Includes index.
    ISBN-10: 1-56924-275-5
    1. Dogs—Training. I. Title.
    SF431.S73 2007
    636.7'0887—dc22

                                                    2006031076

ISBN-13: 978-1-56924-275-9

9 8 7 6 5 4 3 2 1
Designed by Pauline Neuwirth, Neuwirth and Associates, Inc.

Printed in the United States of America

TO MY DAUGHTER ROSALEE

"He who strives unceasingly upward, him can we save."
—Johann Wolfgang von Goethe

Contents

Introduction:
Letting the Dog Decide

My journey to the heart of dogness, a journey not from light to darkness but from fear and confusion to understanding, began when I was five years old. One warm, sunny summer afternoon in front of my family's suburban house, I was playing with a group of other children when a neighbor's large Collie suddenly attacked. The dog lunged and grabbed a child by the face and pulled him to the ground. I was that child.

I began to scream and fight to free myself from the dog's grip. I could clearly see down its throat, and the stink of its breath remains with me to this day. The more I fought, the harder the dog bit down on my head. The Collie had begun to drag me down the street by the face when its owner heard my screams, raced out, and forced the dog to set me free.

From that day forward I lived in abject terror of dogs. Even the smallest breed could freeze me like stone by staring and barking in my direction. During the next few years it was not unusual for my parents to have to send my older brother out to find me when I failed to return home from school. Invariably he would discover me standing stock-still, crying, with a dog circling about, amusing himself at my expense.

In sports, from baseball and tennis to football and ice hockey, I had no fear, and so the day finally came when I could no longer tolerate my unreasoning terror of dogs. In chess and hockey, my father had taught me that to overcome an opponent, one must study his habits, thoughts, and dispositions to discover his strengths and weaknesses. I therefore set out to learn all I could about dogs.

I read every book about dogs that I could lay my hands on. I hung around dog kennels and volunteered at the local SPCA. I made friends with, and did cleanup and odd jobs for, those vets who recognized my keen interest in dogs and animals in general. Along the way I discovered that the Collie who bit me on the face was trying to elicit a submissive response. Dogs "face bite" because puppies have a natural reflexive response to pressure on the head and face. If you squeeze a puppy's head, it will go limp. This makes for quick, effective discipline in the pack. If I had gone limp instead of screaming and thrashing about, the Collie would have stopped biting me.

By the time I was in my mid-teens, I was taking on dog-training assignments. My methods were "old school" and my results were more a result of my passion for the work than my technique. Then came a change in my life that led to a whole new approach to training dogs. I began to work with emotionally disturbed children for the British Columbia Department of Social Services.

During this time I was exposed to all manner of ideas about modifying behavior. The most important idea was to refrain from making judgments about a person's behavior until I understood that person's point of view. For example, I worked with many angry, aggressive boys who had been diagnosed as misogynistic. Indeed, these boys did have a violent dislike of women, but on working with them I discovered that they had all been severely abused—sexually, physically, and/or emotionally—by their mothers and other women who had power over them. Meanwhile, society was perfectly willing to put these dead-end kids in jail for the rest of their lives, without ever recognizing the cause of their dysfunction and treating them for it.

With these boys (I could also cite cases of girls whose dysfunction was caused by abuse by men, of boys abused by men, and of girls abused by women), I learned that real change must come from within; it must be volunteered. My job was to provide guidance and fertile ground for change and clear direction, so that the boys could see how they hurt themselves with their own behavior. You can't beat or coerce change out of a person or a dog. That only makes the person or dog more resistant and angry.

My success rate with disturbed children was very high, but I eventually succumbed to the burnout that inevitably accompanies such work.

Armed with a completely new perspective, I returned to the training of dogs. I began breeding and showing German Shepherd Dogs and soon gained a reputation as a trainer who could turn dogs that no one else could handle into champions. This work spread to all breeds.

The random, subjective nature of the judging at conformation dog shows led me to a type of competition where a measurable score could be attained. I found myself comfortably at home in the highly technical German dog sport of Schutzhund, which involves tracking, obedience, and protection. Through books, videos, and personal contact, I learned from the best trainers in European dog sports. During this time I was constantly training dogs for the public, usually through referrals from veterinarians. I developed a reputation as a trainer who could handle the most difficult dogs, to the point that most of my clients came to me only after failing over and over with other trainers.

Whenever a dog was brought to me, I was told in one way or another, "It won't behave." But as I always discovered and explained, it would have been more accurate to say, "The dog can't behave, because its training has not taught it how to escape its own fear and anxiety."

One of my clients at this time was a woman in Washington State who bred and handled show dogs. She had a beautiful male sporting dog that would shiver and urinate whenever a male judge approached him. The woman brought the dog to my place, and I agreed to work with him. That evening my wife, Laurie, fed and walked the dog with no problem. The next morning I went to get him out of the kennel and he bit me.

Well, I was none too happy about that. Clients sometimes avoid mentioning all the facts about a dog, but I like to know if a dog will bite, just for my own safety. I went in and phoned her and blasted her. She admitted that she had been too embarrassed to tell me that her boyfriend, who was jealous of the time she lavished on her dogs every weekend, would take this particular dog out and play ball with him, then sucker him into the electric cattle fence they had on their farm. This explained the dog's biting behavior all right, just as the abuse the disturbed boys had suffered from some women explained their misogyny.

I decided to continue working with the dog, and at first Laurie had to get him out of the kennel because he was frightened of me. Once he was out of the kennel, he wouldn't bite. Slowly but surely he started to trust me, and we built a good relationship.

The dog had a good name for a sporting dog, but I had to change it because his name was "burnt": he feared it through association to being teased into the electric fence. I renamed him Scooter, which the breeder hated. (That was my revenge for her not telling me what the real source of the problem was until after I had been bitten.)

I taught Scooter to "escape" his fear by engaging in positively reinforced show behaviors, which was how I reeducated show dogs. We became the best of friends and I remember him with great fondness. I took him out to show and we did very well. He was a gorgeous young dog, and it was great fun to have a dog so good to compete with. After I completed his championship in Canada, the owner came up and took him back to the United States, where he enjoyed a great career.

Even seriously troubled dogs can be taught, gently and reliably, to escape compulsion in compliance. For about ten years I was the "last chance appeals court lawyer" for aggressive dogs on death row in the Vancouver area. After their owners had taken the dogs to every other trainer around, and no one could help, they brought the dogs to me. Some of the boys I counseled made me think, "This is it, fella. It's either learn to live differently or wind up in jail or dead on the streets." Likewise, I looked at these dogs, male and female, and thought, "This is it, friend, do or die." There was nothing inherently wrong with most of these dogs, just like with most of the boys I worked with, and they usually "trained out" fine. I am proud to say that very few of these dogs had to go back to death row.

But being put in the position over and over again of having to save perfectly good dogs that had been damaged by human beings' mistreatment created an underlying tension. I found myself unable to stop thinking about all the dogs that are put down for no fault of their own, and I do not do this type of work anymore.

Nowadays I devote my training time to developing dogs for technical work such as tracking, search and rescue, explosives and cadaver detection, and protection; training a small number of companion dogs for private clients; and sharing my methods with average dog owners through seminars and workshops.

Throughout my experiences with dogs, I have sought to refine my understanding of them and to design a gentle, reliable training method that can be used successfully by anyone, anywhere, with any dog. This book is the culmination of that effort. With the average dog owner in mind, I have written it to provide a complete—and completely gentle—training system based on a correct understanding of the dog's psychology. My training system accepts the dog's independent will, insatiable curiosity, and strong instinctual drives, not as problems that must be controlled, but as fortunate natural attributes that can aid learning. It shows exactly how training succeeds or fails through the interaction of the dog and the trainer, and it makes the dog an active participant in the training process rather than a stubborn, resistant subject.

The cornerstone of my method is based on the psychological effect on the dog of benevolent eye contact and a combination of covert control and overt positive reinforcement in three five-minute training sessions a day. The convenience of training sessions that are short enough to cram into a busy day is a lucky by-product of the fact that short training sessions are more effective than long ones.

There are people whose individual and family lives don't leave fifteen good minutes a day free to devote to dog training. You might take a moment to ask yourself whether you really can, or cannot, give your dog three five-minute training sessions a day. If you can't, you shouldn't get a dog. But if you can, that's all the time you'll need.

HUMAN BEINGS MISTREAT dogs through poor training because they fail to understand their true nature. Dogs have no morality and no ethics. They behave in accordance with their evolution as opportunistic predators and scavengers, omnivores, and pack animals.

A dog is incapable of understanding the reason for your actions. The language of most dog-training books glosses over this in the frequent use of the word "correction" and advice on how to administer "corrections" of the dog's behavior with the choke chain or pinch collar. The word has a moral and ethical connotation that does not apply to dogs and misleads us if we use it in relation to training, because it implies that the dog will understand why we are hurting it, as you would understand why you were being "corrected" by your parents, for example, for being rude to someone.

This will never happen. The dog just sees that you are putting it in pain. It never understands why.

Nearly all problems with dogs occur because people expect them to behave like something other than dogs and are disappointed when they don't. If we all expected our dogs to urinate on the rug, defecate in the corner, steal the chicken, dig up the yard, or bark all day, as dogs will, we would train them not to do these things and everything would be fine.

Dog-training books and dog owners commonly speak of problems with a dog in terms of its "bad habits." Because dogs can only engage in behaviors that are canine in nature, what this really means is that some natural canine behaviors are unwanted by us. It is also worth mentioning here that dogs do not repeat unsuccessful behaviors. So these unwanted behaviors have brought the dog reward in some way. They have been reinforced, or they would not have been repeated.

For example, barking and chewing, both natural to the dog, dissipate nervous energy and bring some satisfaction to it. Digging out of the yard sets it free to roam with other dogs in the neighborhood and enjoy their company. This freedom is particularly reinforcing if the dog is left alone all day. Ripping into the garbage brings the promise of some unearned snacks. Nipping children produces flight, which raises status and offers other satisfactions like dropped ice cream cones and peanut butter sandwiches. A dog that can take food from other creatures is powerful indeed in the world of dogs.

Visit any public park frequented by dog owners and you will see how desperately a better way of training is needed. You will see dogs pulling frantically on their leashes to pursue their own interests and escape their owners' commands. You will see the dogs' owners yanking violently on the other end of the leash, dragging their unhappy, resentful, fearful, and/or aggressive dogs this way and that and inflicting physical and psychological pain on them every step of the way. You will see dogs running away from their owners with every fiber of their beings, so that they can root in the trash, chase squirrels, or play or fight with other dogs—anything except go back on the hated leash for more mistreatment by people who do not understand them. The vast majority of these dog owners and their dogs love each other, but they can realize only a fraction of their potential for a good relationship because of the woeful state of dog training.

Visit any dog pound or animal shelter and you will see the need for better training even more poignantly displayed. Hundreds of thousands of dogs are put down in North America every year because they have been abandoned in frustration, or at the behest of the authorities, by owners whose training efforts have failed completely.

It does not have to be that way. If you learn how to let your dog decide to do the right thing, the two of you can enjoy an endlessly rewarding relationship.

Letting the dog decide may sound like an abdication of responsibility, a cop-out that ignores the violence that dogs are capable of inflicting. After all, isn't the point of training to get the dog to do what the owner wants, to obey commands and do what it is told?

But as in Zen archery, where master archers say they simply "pull the bow and let the arrow find its target," letting the dog decide is, in counterintuitive fact, the only route to willing obedience. If we shape training situations and reinforce desired behaviors appropriately, we never have to command or force dogs to do anything. That is a path of inevitably diminishing returns. If we let the dogs decide, they will do anything we ask eagerly, because they have seen for themselves that it is in their best interest to do so.

The fundamental problem with current training techniques is that they shut down the dog's mind or fail to empower it effectively. My method keeps the dog's mind open to learning and discovery, and there is nothing like seeing a confident, curious dog decide that the winning strategy is to do what you want it to do. The thrill of seeing a dog open its mind to the training that is necessary for its well-being and safety is what keeps me excited about training after countless training sessions with countless dogs. It is a thrill that every dog owner can experience with my methods.

Let the Dog Decide

· PART ONE ·

Preparing to Train

To the Dog's Understanding:
Why Training Succeeds or Fails

To train any animal effectively, we need to appreciate that animal's distinctive natural attributes, especially how it understands the world and how it learns. And then we need to follow a training system that fits those attributes, rather than fights them.

Any illusions we have about an animal are going to interfere with its training. Unfortunately, thanks to Walt Disney films and other forms of entertainment, we have some strange ideas about the dog. These illusions and incorrect assumptions prevent us from getting where we want to go with the dog.

When we refuse to accept dogs as they are, we turn our backs on the best possibilities for training them. We will be much better off to use what dogs offer us, rather than try to impose an artificial system on them.

Dogs in the Wild

DOGS EVOLVED IN the wild as omnivorous, opportunistic, scavenging, predatory, and highly social animals that live in a pack led by an alpha breeding pair. Alpha dominance over the rest of the pack is often noted in dog-training books, but it is almost equally often misinterpreted, insofar as its implications for training are concerned (see, "Do You Really Want to Be Alpha?" later in the chapter).

In addition to their distinctive social life, dogs have a well-defined developmental process. Puppies go through a period of imprinting, and experience their most profound learning, between seven and eleven weeks of age. During this period, puppies learn to read the subtle body language that dogs use to communicate with each other, and they begin patterns of behavior that will last a lifetime.

Puppyhood lasts from birth to three years of age. Throughout this book I use the words puppy and dog interchangeably, except where I specifically refer to older dogs. Technically this is incorrect, because "dog" is a gendered term. Professional dog people and animal behaviorists use the terms "dog" and "bitch" for male and female animals, respectively, without any moral implications.

Based on observations of both domestic dogs and wild dogs, including wolves, the original source of all domestic dog breeds, scientists have demonstrated that dogs are self-interested creatures. Unlike the image presented in Walt Disney films, dogs are not benevolent.

This is not to deny the powerful emotional bond that can grow up between person and dog, transcending immediate self-interest, but to establish it on its true and only foundation. Dogs want to win access to resources, and they have no morality or ethics in pursuit of that goal. They will quickly adopt any behavior that succeeds in winning resources, and they will just as quickly abandon any behavior that fails to do so.

Dogs' determination to win access to resources manifests itself in countless adaptations to challenging environments around the world. Behaviors of genetically identical wolves living above and below the Arctic tree line offer a fascinating example of this.

In the forests south of the tree line, the wolves are solitary hunters of small game. They will take deer if they get lucky, but mostly they prey, in a stalk-and-pounce fashion, on the lemmings, field mice, rabbits, and so on that abound in the forest.

On the tundra north of the tree line, the exact same wolves genetically hunt big game, the caribou, in a pack. Male and female members of the pack hunt together like the Oakland Raiders play football. There are wide receivers, fast dogs that flank the prey. There are linebackers, dogs that come in from behind and harry the prey on the hip. And there are linemen, dogs that tackle the prey and bring it down. These jobs never change in the pack.

The wolves above the tree line have specialized jobs in a well-organized, collective hunt. The wolves below the tree line still live together in packs, but as hunters they are multitasking generalists that hunt solo.

Dogs and People

WHEN DOGS BEGAN making a place for themselves in the human environment, they brought along their natural attributes, especially their endless adaptability. They used these qualities to become human beings' partners in a collective struggle for survival.

Human beings then took over the evolution of dogs, selectively breeding them to hunt game, herd livestock, guard the hearth, and haul cargo. Ultimately that led to the breeding of dogs for all the purposes of work, play, and aesthetic refinement that are reflected in today's breeds, from the German Shepherd Dog to the Lhasa Apso. Before that process could advance very far, however, people and dogs had to learn how to work together and people had to develop effective ways of training dogs to perform varied tasks.

Dogs brought their immense observational skills, as well as their more obvious physical gifts, to their interactions with people. They quickly learned to read human beings' body language as well as that of other dogs. Modern science has not yet fully plumbed the extent of this ability, which enables dogs to detect a heart attack or stroke hours before it occurs and to scent the onset of cancer months before high-tech medical diagnostics can find it.

For their part, people learned that it paid to observe dogs closely to detect their underlying moods, behaviors, and interests. They saw how dogs experimented to identify successful behaviors, and they noted the dynamic learning ability of puppies. They saw, too, how dogs used their observational skills to anticipate steps in training.

Over countless generations of hunting and herding with dogs, our ancestors recognized that the most effective training methods were generally the least forceful, and the ones that put the dog in a good mood; that the more a dog discovered for itself, the more it could learn; and that the best training empowered the dog's own decision-making ability. People found, in short, that dogs would cheerfully do anything they were asked, even to the point of sacrificing their lives to protect their human masters, so long as they clearly understood what they were expected to do and received positive reinforcement for doing it.

Direct feedback from the premodern environment optimized people's treatment of dogs. If people confused their dogs, were too hard on them, or otherwise behaved in a way that undermined the dogs' ability to work confidently, cheerfully, and efficiently, the people suffered.

They lost valuable livestock to predators and thieves, or their hunts failed and they did not bring in enough game to feed their families, among other calamities.

As human lifestyles have changed in the modern world, a correct knowledge of dogs and how to train them has almost disappeared. Once widely shared, it now survives mainly where people continue to work with dogs in traditional ways, such as in Scottish sheepherding communities. The paradox is that as we have migrated from herding and farming to living in cities and towns, asking dogs to do less and less for us, we have become harsher and harsher to them. In so doing, we have lost control of dogs as pets and companions.

What most of us need and want our dogs to do today is trivial by comparison to what our ancestors asked of them. Sit, stay, down, walk calmly on the leash, come when called—these are simple ABCs for the dog, which can still excel at difficult jobs such as herding livestock, search and rescue, explosives detection, and service to the blind. Yet in our modern urban and suburban lives, the pet dog has become a problem we can't handle.

The average pet dog refuses to sit, stay, down, walk calmly on the leash, or come when called. Instead, it urinates on the rug, eats the family dinner, barks and howls all day, destroys furniture, jumps up on visitors, runs off to root in a neighbor's trash or hide from its owners, digs up the garden, or shows aggression to other dogs or people, including family members. The most underreported animal incidents in North America are of dogs that bite their owners.

These behaviors frustrate dog owners and their families; put dogs at risk from speeding cars and other tragedies, such as a one-way trip to the dog pound or animal shelter; and in the worst cases may injure or even kill people, including a dog-owning family's own children. Instead of cooperation between dogs and people, there is a hopeless, costly battle of wills.

The first thing to realize about dogs in the modern world is that they have lost none of their instinctual drives, adaptability, observational skill, and ability to master complex tasks. When people seek my help with their dogs, I often hear scenarios like this:

"I've been trying to get Fluffy to sit for a year for a cookie, and sometimes she sits for a cookie, but not always. However, Fluffy quickly learned that Thursday is garbage day, and she figured out how to get out of the yard on garbage day in order to feast from the garbage cans in the alley. I built a fence, and Fluffy jumped over it. I built a higher fence, and Fluffy dug under it. So I put wire mesh in the ground below the fence. And then Fluffy learned to open the gate."

How is it that Fluffy responded to a year of being taught to sit with a random performance, but after one foray into the garbage, she figured out ever more difficult ways to repeat the experience? Well, there's something different about the learning processes involved.

With the garbage as opposed to the sit on command, Fluffy thought it all out herself. No one said no; no one stopped her. She had all the time in the world to think her way determinedly through the problem. And at the end of the problem, she didn't get a dry little cookie ("That again? I've been eating those for a year.") as she did when she sat for her owner. Instead, she got leftover pizza and everything else that was in the garbage cans.

The process by which Fluffy got out of the yard and into the garbage produced huge rewards. It's pretty clear how Fluffy learns best. The method Fluffy used is the method that works. She won big on her own terms. She came away with a picture of her thoughts, her process, her experiments as winning reward, and no one told her what to do and when to do it.

What we want to do is replicate the system and the thought processes by which Fluffy figured out how to get what she wanted. We want to present the dog in training with a situation where it has to think out how to solve the problem itself.

Let's look at the two main training methods available today, alpha-dominance-based classical conditioning with a leash attached to a choke chain or pinch collar on the one hand and operant conditioning with a clicker on the other, to see how they compare with Fluffy's own discoveries.

Classical Conditioning

LET'S SAY HYPOTHETICALLY that I'm your boss and I want you to sit down at your desk to work. If every time you get up, I come over and push you back down and then give you a cookie, you may sit and eat the cookie, but eventually you will start to feel resentful. It's not your idea to sit, perhaps it's uncomfortable at the moment. If I push hard, you may even be hurt when you slam into your chair.

In behavioral terms, this scenario subjects you to overt, painful control in return for a negligible positive reinforcement. This is exactly what happens in classical conditioning with a choke chain or pinch collar, the mainstream of North American and British dog training.

In plain language, classical conditioning is punishment-based training, using the leash and choke chain or pinch collar as an overt means of control and punishment. One of the saddest things for dog owners and their dogs is how books that claim to teach a gentle method of training gloss over the discomfort that a choke chain inflicts on a dog.

Here is a typical example of what is found in many books on dog training for teaching the dog to sit:

Put the dog in the heel position. Say, "Sit." Pull up on the choke chain until the dog sits. When it sits, say, "Good dog," and give it a pet and/or a cookie.

This method appears to make sense, as we teach children in much the same way, but there is a great difference between a child's understanding and a dog's. Training the dog to sit like this creates a negative association with the word "sit" because the word and the choking pain happen simultaneously. Even worse, it creates a negative association with the human being who has inflicted the pain and with training in general. This kind of advice is usually couched in terms of the owner's acting as the alpha pack leader that the dog must obey or rue the consequences.

Repeat this lesson only a few times and the dog's response to the word "sit" will forever be associated with pain and the owner. The dog will be reluctant to give the sit and never give it outside the length of a leash from the owner. When I train a dog that has previously suffered punishment-based training, I have to use entirely new words to cue behaviors, because "sit," "stay," "down," and "come," and probably the dog's name as well, have been burned for the dog for life by the negative associations it has learned to make with them.

Notice how in the preceding example a negative reinforcer, pulling on the choke chain, precedes and overrides the positive reinforcer, the praise and the food treat. That can only be deeply confusing to a dog's understanding. Moreover, it is vital to notice that with classical conditioning techniques, the dog has no escape from the negative reinforcer. It will be hurt no matter what it does and no matter how quickly it responds to your wishes.

An expert in animal behavioral psychology might object that this typical "sit" example does not show the pitfalls of using classical conditioning but of misusing it. I agree. But no book can teach you how to separate negative reinforcement from positive reinforcement while using a choke chain or pinch collar for classical conditioning, because it takes lengthy trial and error. In fact, most experts agree that it takes about ten years to learn to use a leash and choke chain or pinch collar properly, at exactly the right instant and without excessive force.

The Difference a Collar Makes.

CHOKE CHAINS, CHOKE collars, and pinch collars come in many varieties, from simple slip leads, which may be made of metal or assorted natural and synthetic materials, to collars with inward-facing metal prongs, with or without rubber tips. As training tools and control devices, choke chains and pinch collars share a fundamental flaw: their use almost inevitably leads to inadvertent and extreme "corrections," which hurt and confuse the dog.

Pinch collars and choke chains are supposed to mimic the way a mother dog nips her puppies to keep them in line. But a mother dog never nips her puppies by mistake. And she bites with precise control.

The choke chain and the pinch collar are both hard to control, however. First, it is difficult to apply them at exactly the right instant and to avoid applying them by accident, so that the dog associates the pain with a behavior you are trying to "correct" rather than with something else, although even then the dog will never understand why you are punishing it in this way. Second, it is difficult to control the force of the choke chain and the pinch collar. Perhaps even more with the pinch collar than the choke chain, it is easy to inflict significant pain without meaning to do so.

Expert trainers require years of practice to use choke chains and pinch collars effectively, and in some circumstances even an expert may not be able to avoid misusing them. For example, suppose you are walking a dog along the street on a choke or pinch collar, when the dog is startled by squealing tires and blaring car horns. Or suppose you are walking the dog when it sees a beloved family member or friend approaching. The dog's natural response—to flee from danger or rush forward to greet a friend—will result in its being violently choked or pinched by the collar, and thus in its making an association that may have dire consequences in the future. Such inadvertent lessons occur frequently with choke and pinch collars, making them a poor choice for both training and general management of the dog.

Another problem with choke and pinch collars is that the more they are used, the less effective they become. The dog becomes hardened to the choke or pinch collar tightening around its neck, and the more assertive and strong-willed the dog is, the more likely it will experience this sensation as a stimulus rather than a "correction."

An expert trainer can make effective use of a choke chain or pinch collar in a carefully controlled situation that takes into account the limitations of the tool and the dog's individual temperament and disposition. Using the tool effectively requires absolutely precise timing. The trainer must plan exactly how and when to trigger an undesirable behavior in the dog; apply appropriate pressure on the choke chain or pinch collar at the instant the dog displays the behavior; and release the pressure the instant the dog stops the behavior. There must be no inadvertent tightening of the choke chain or pinch collar, and no overuse of them.

Outside such limited use by experts, it is best to abandon the choke chain and pinch collar, along with all punishment-based training, and to use the flat collar for dog training and handling. Greater control of the dog can be achieved covertly or overtly, but in any case painlessly, through the respective use of long lines attached to the flat collar or the Halti brand head collar for walks (see Chapter 2).

If we try to look at training from the dog's point of view, we can see how unnecessary choke chains and pinch collars are. We need only make sure that the dog fails when trying out behaviors we do not want, and succeeds when it engages in behaviors we do want, to create a positive training relationship between the dog and ourselves. Adding discomfort to the mix through the use of poorly controlled force in the form of the pinch and choke collars, which negatively affect the dog's happiness and sense of safety and security in our presence, is simply counterproductive.

Yet dog training books, videos, and classes commonly tell the novice dog owner to begin training by putting a choke chain on a little puppy, precisely when it is most impressionable. If you go to puppy obedience class, the first lesson is usually to take your nice, friendly, happy, devoted puppy, put a choke chain or pinch collar on its neck, attach a leash, and then take the leash in your hand and start walking in a tight circle. If the puppy balks, or looks off to the side, the instructor tells you to pull on the leash and tighten the choke chain around its neck.

Because you understand the exercise, you think that the dog should understand it. But if you ever see a dog walking in a tight circle by itself, it is likely ill, perhaps rabid. You're asking your puppy to do something unnatural that it cannot understand.

As you're walking around in a circle with your happy little puppy, it gets distracted by another puppy.

"Oh, look at that puppy over there," the dog thinks.

Bang! Following instructions, you pull sharply on the choke chain.

Now your puppy thinks, "Oh! What was that?" A little bit of fear and worry has suddenly entered its mind. After about twenty jerks, the dog has figured out you want to walk in a circle and it doesn't think much of you at all.

Then the instructor tells you to walk with the puppy in a straight line and when it gets in front of you, turn about face and—bang!—pull on the leash.

"What's going on?" the puppy wonders, now seriously frightened. "We were just walking in a circle, now you go rushing back the other way, and does my neck ever hurt."

Not being a moron, and being very good at reading body language, the dog sees your hands on the leash and makes an association. It sees that when you pull with your hands, its neck hurts. It sees, too, that you offer it no escape from that pain.

Because the dog is such an adaptable creature, it's going to forgive you up to a point. Sooner or later, however, the dog will conclude that there is no positive result to your behavior. Many people come to me saying, "Bruno was first in obedience class. At six months old, he was perfect. Now he's a year old and he's an utter terror."

That's because the system has broken down. The feedback the dog has gotten has not changed. Every time the dog acts in its own best interests, it sees your hands move and feels a negative result. No creature is going to enjoy that.

Misused overt control produces discomfort, which in turn produces resentment, because it does not allow for the dog's self-directed participation and does not enable it to escape compulsion. The dog suffers and fears for itself at the hands of its owner, the person it trusted the most. Punishment-based training destroys the bond between dog and owner and drives the dog into defense, because the dog needs to protect itself. Self-defense is the dog's natural, God-given right. And if the dog has high status because of its dominant temperament, it will defend its right to have some dignity as well.

When a dog goes into defense, it has three possible responses: submission, avoidance, and aggression. In relation to the dog's owner, they will usually come in the same order. The first strategy is to submit. Dogs have worked things out with each other that if there is conflict between the big guy and the little guy, the little guy will submit by lying down on the ground, tucking its tail under its rear, whimpering, and/or urinating. A dog should never be punished for spontaneous urination. The dog is saying, "Please don't hurt me. I am not a threat."

If the dog tries any of these behaviors in puppy class, the instructor will say, "Get that dog up and moving and don't let it do that." The response to the dog's honest submissive behavior is to choke it. But the dog is just trying to tell you that it wants to submit to be spared further pain.

Submission doesn't work, so the dog tries its next method, avoidance, which fundamentally means, "Run away." For the pet dog, this involves staying outside its owner's area of influence. This is the distance over which you have taught the dog that you have control of it with your bare hand or with a leash in your hand.

Soon the dog will refuse to recall to a position right in front of you or will run off when you call. This happens because getting close to you is where discomfort happens. You've taken the area where the dog should feel safest and made it the area where the dog feels least safe.

The frequent occurrence is that Bruno won't come when it's time to leave the dog park. First the owner tries screaming at Bruno and then begging him. So Bruno finally relents, and when he gets into the area of influence, he crawls cautiously with his ears down and his tail under his rear to his owner, who at the first opportunity grabs him roughly, snaps the leash on the choke chain or pinch collar, and hauls him off. Bruno's reward for the recall is that he is abused.

Bruno has no idea what's wrong. All he knows is that his owner is crazy: "He takes me to the park, and then he gets furious at me."

Classical conditioning with a leash and choke chain makes you an incomprehensible creature to the dog. So the dog uses avoidance in defense of itself until it exhausts this technique. And then especially if the dog is genetically predisposed to it, the only natural response left is aggression, which properly understood is almost always a form of flight forward.

The dog may not feel it can use its aggression on the trainer, especially if that person is acting like an alpha dog. It will then look for little kids and others who are vulnerable. And before you know it, the dog is biting the kids or the kids' friends. Aggression rises and rises and rises.

Many European dogs like the Belgian Malinois have what is called civil defense bred in them. If you try handling them incorrectly, they will bite you without hesitation. All dogs will show aggression if they feel trapped and are concerned enough for their safety. And some dogs will show civil defense.

This happens all the time, but as I already mentioned, it goes unreported. People don't want to go into the doctor's office and admit that they were behaving in such a way that their own dog bit them.

It is nearly impossible for classical conditioning with an overt control device, such as a leash attached to a choke chain or pinch collar, to instill willing obedience in a dog. As soon as you unsnap the leash and take off the choke chain, the dog does whatever it wants. It can see plainly that you are dependent on the leash.

When the leash is attached to the choke chain and you have it in your hand, the dog does not volunteer anything. It acts as you wish because you're forcing it. The dog's true will is functioning under the surface, and the only thing that prevents the dog from expressing its will is your attentive hold on the leash.

Many training manuals based on classical conditioning never bother to ask if the dog sits eagerly or reluctantly, if its ears are up and its tail is wagging and it looks happy and eager, or if its ears are down and its tail is under its belly and it looks uncomfortable and frightened. Training is described in terms of human education, as if dogs were people, and uses methods that alienate the dog by ignoring its true nature. It is no good if the dog responds under control of choker or pinch collar and leash if we are at the same time unwittingly creating an aversion to the very behavior we are teaching.

Even the best use of classical conditioning alone will almost always produce a dog that can only respond to instructions rigidly, by rote, and that obeys only when it is leashed or under the direct control of an "alpha" human being whose willingness to inflict pain is clear to the dog.

Do You Really Want
to Be Alpha?

SO MANY DOG training books insist that the trainer should be the dog's alpha pack leader that it is worth looking closely at what this involves. In fact, being alpha to your dog is a losing proposition for both of you.

The reason is that among dogs, being alpha is a tenuous, temporary position. In wolf and wild-dog packs, an alpha breeding pair dominate the pack. But this does not mean that life in the pack is peaceful. Beneath the alpha male and female, the other dogs are constantly wrangling for position, with the stronger dogs lording it over the weaker ones.

When the alpha male in the pack shows any weakness because of age or injury, the younger males drive him out or literally tear him to pieces. And then the strongest of these dogs compete to become the new alpha male. The alpha female faces the same fate sooner or later. After an average of two or three years at the top of the pack hierarchy, every alpha is replaced by a younger dog.

If you reduce your human status to that of an alpha dog in your dog's eyes, you are condemning yourself to trying to keep the dog permanently in submission. Every dog, like every other creature with a mind of its own, resents enforced, prolonged submission. As time goes on, dogs with temperaments that place them below the midpoint of the spectrum from submissive to dominant will gradually shut down and withdraw into themselves, while those at the midpoint or higher end of the spectrum will grow more, not less, inclined to test your alpha status.

Meanwhile, neither of these two types of dog will respect or listen to anyone else in the household. Some dog training books say that everyone in the family should be alpha to the dog. This makes no sense to a dog. In a dog's world, there can never be more than one alpha and no alpha is permanent.

Among the most common problems that people ask me to help them with is when one member of the household, usually the husband or father, has become alpha to the dog and no one else can control it. Either the husband brings the dog to me, complaining that it's driving his wife crazy and terrorizing the kids when he's not home, or his wife arrives with a similar complaint.

Unlike dogs trained with alpha and dominance methods, dogs trained by my method are responsive to all family members. Here is a powerful working dog showing total responsiveness to ten-year-old Rosalee.

The same powerful working dog happily giving the most submissive of all gestures, the down, to the smallest and weakest family member.

When the alpha's away, the dog will play. And dogs play rough. They play like professional football players play football. Alpha dominance training can easily create havoc, and even tragedy, in a household.

In farming families that still rely on working dogs, the members of the family are not alpha to the dog. The dog does not submit to the human beings as it would to a pack leader; it respects and defers to them as we would to a wise elder. Being a dog's beloved master is something far different from being the alpha it must submit to or rue the consequences. If you want a dog's deference and respect, rather than its unwilling submission, you do not want to be alpha.

Classical conditioning can be a formula for producing fearful, anxious, resentful dogs that can no longer think for themselves.

There is a poignant story out of Scotland that I remember from when I was a young trainer. The Scots train some of the greatest sheepdogs in the world, and the best Scottish trainers use a very kind, open-minded, respectful process to develop these dogs. Herding dogs have traditionally been trained the world over in ways that empower their minds, because to protect livestock, they must literally think on the move, making innumerable independent decisions in response to unpredictable events such as the weather and the approach of predators or thieves. Scottish sheep farmers, for example, cannot rely on physical control or psychological intimidation, when their dogs are working a quarter of a mile away.

As an experiment, however, one top Scottish trainer decided to train a dog with classical conditioning. As this punishment-based method requires, the trainer used strict compulsion whenever the dog made a mistake or gave an alternate response to a signal. This produced a dog that was unthinkingly obedient to specific commands.

One day the trainer put the dog in a down–stay while he went and opened a cattle gate. The cattle were spooked from the enclosure and charged out the gate. True to its classical conditioning, the dog did not break the stay and was trampled to death. The trainer vowed that he would never again be so foolish or inhumane as to train a dog in this manner.

Operant Conditioning— Clicking to the Next Stage

IN THE PAST twenty-five years, a second stream of dog training methods has appeared in North America: the operant conditioning techniques of Karen Pryor. She was a student of B. F. Skinner, the man who defined "operant conditioning."

In the hands of Pryor and other students of Skinner, operant conditioning evolved into a way to manipulate marine mammals during psychological studies of behavior. This method involves no compulsion, no force, whatsoever. Pryor saw the possibility of using this method on dogs, and she wrote *Don't Shoot the Dog: The New Art of Teaching and Training*, spawning a school of so-called clicker trainers, because of their use of a clicker, or in Skinner's terms, a conditioned reinforcer.

The sound of the clicker helps build an association in the dog's mind between an obedience behavior and the provision of a food treat.

Karen Pryor and the clicker trainers who have followed her lead deserve great credit for rediscovering and sharing the knowledge that it is possible to teach dogs behaviors without inflicting pain on them. Operant techniques are invaluable if used correctly, and they have a prominent place in my training system. They have long been used, with different conditioned reinforcers than a clicker (such as whistles and calls), by trainers of herding and other working dogs to teach them positive associations with desired behaviors. Any number of things can be used as a conditioned reinforcer, but the ultimate conditioned reinforcer is the safety and respect, or the lack thereof, that dogs feel from the people training them.

There is a vast gap between teaching dogs an association, however, and training a response that they will reliably give on cue. Operant conditioning alone will not produce a dog that sits, downs, walks calmly on the leash, and comes when called. Like classical conditioning, but in a very different way, operant conditioning with a clicker cannot train a dog to escape compulsion into compliance, and it cannot empower the dog to make good decisions on its own, as sheepherding and other work and service dogs must do, and as we want our pets to do when we are not watching them. Animals subjected to gentle operant conditioning, including dogs, dolphins in marine parks, and tigers and lions in circuses, may still be dangerously aggressive toward people and may even maim or kill them.

In the formal training chapters I describe exactly how to get the most from clickers and other operant teaching tools. But here it's important to note that the clicker shares one drawback with the leash and the choke chain: It is very difficult to time correctly. In using a clicker, you have only milliseconds in which to connect the clicking sound and a food treat with a specific behavior. It easily happens that the dog thus learns something different from what you are trying to teach.

For example, a student trainer once consulted me about a Great Dane that would not recall and sit properly. On viewing a video of one of the dog's training sessions, I saw what the problem was. Because the clicks were not timed precisely—an exceedingly difficult thing for even an experienced trainer—the dog had come to believe that the correct procedure for the recall and sit was to charge in close, rear up on its hind legs to punch the trainer in the stomach with its front legs, and then sit for a treat. There was not an ounce of ill will in the dog; it was doing exactly what it had been conditioned to do with the clicker.

Operant conditioning with a clicker is never directly hurtful to the dog, and Karen Pryor's championing of it represents a great advance over classical conditioning and punishment-based training. But because operant conditioning only teaches associations with the conditioned reinforcer, it cannot train reliable behaviors and develop the dog's own decision-making abilities in unpredictable situations, and thus it can still leave dogs at risk. The dog that only responds to the conditioned reinforcer cannot be called reliably to stay out of the busy street when it has started to chase a squirrel, for example. Operant conditioning is thus only part—but a very important part—of the answer we need to train our dogs gently and reliably.

A Better Way:
Combining Covert Control
with Overt Positive Reinforcement

THE LORE OF the old stockmen, the experience of modern working dog trainers, and the pros and cons of both classical conditioning and operant conditioning all point in the same direction. An effective dog training system will do the following:

- Always proceed in step with the dog's understanding, and never force the dog to do anything it does not comprehend.
- Take account of the dog's distinctive developmental process and the influence of its moods on its behavior.
- Keep the dog free to choose reward and escape from discomfort in accord with its own wishes.
- Clearly separate positive reinforcement and negative reinforcement in the dog's mind, and never give the dog reason to associate discomfort with the trainer's behavior.
- Preserve and enhance the dog's ability to decide on the appropriate action in unpredictable circumstances.

In reference to the capacity of the dog to make correct decisions under difficult circumstances, a revealing incident occurred with a young German Shepherd named Tiggie that I was protection training.

I had been working her in a scenario where my helper, "the bad guy," would approach the closed back gate of my yard and rattle around a bit to alert the dog to his presence. Tiggie would bark as a warning not to enter. The helper would then open the gate and try to force his way into the yard. As soon as he stepped through the gate, Tiggie would rush in and bite his padded sleeve, driving him back out into the alley, then release his arm and return to me.

The next afternoon I was out in the yard working in my garden at the side of the house, out of sight of the back gate. I was on my knees weeding, and Tiggie was lying placidly on the grass some ten feet away. Suddenly out of the corner of my eye I saw a blur of black and tan streak past. I jumped up to see Tiggie's rear end disappear around the corner of the house, and I ran to the corner just in time to see Tiggie targeting my neighbor's son, who had come into the yard to retrieve his lacrosse ball. He was standing just inside the half-open gate exactly as my helper had been the day before.

My heart sunk. I had no time to call Tiggie off, as she was on him in a heartbeat and had all the justification in the world to bite. The boy stood frozen in terror as he recognized Tiggie's intentions. At the last moment she stopped her attack, sniffed at his arm and leg, wagged her tail and returned to me. I praised her without reservation for her decision not to bite.

I reminded my neighbor's son, once again, never to enter my yard without permission. When I went back in my house, I thought long and hard about the training process that had allowed Tiggie to make her own decision about what was truly a threat and whether or not she should bite. Only a dog who possessed a calm, clear mind and felt no pressure to bite could have made such a decision. I felt very grateful for her excellent temperament and disposition and for the time and care I had put into her training as a protection dog. This certainly made clear that dogs could make good decisions on their own when they were trained in a way that left them with the capacity to do so.

What I am talking about here is that when dogs are trained through force and "absolutes," they are left with no alternatives outside the trained behavior. When the dog has been trained to choose for itself, it is still obedient, but all of its individual wits and character remain intact. It has not been robbed of its sense of self and turned into an automaton. It is not an unwilling slave; it is a partner who shares in the experience with its handler.

As a search and rescue dog in Washington state, Greta works tracking, cadaver, and evidence for the city police department, county sheriff's department, tribal police, and the FBI. She also holds the American Kennel Club working titles of Canine Good Citizen, Tracking Dog, and Companion Dog.

Rhime is certified by the Royal Canadian Mounted Police in both tracking and searching. Her titles include Working Dog, Search and Rescue, and Companion Dog, where she twice scored the highest points in trial.

Penny holds the American Kennel Club working titles of Canine Good Citizen, Tracking Dog, and Companion Dog. Her skills in search and rescue, explosive detection, and evidence detection have proven invaluable to both the local community and law enforcement.

You will be able to achieve this with your dog by following the training system explained here, which combines covert control of the dog with overt positive reinforcement. The next chapter gives an overview of the system and how to follow it.

Let the **Dog** Decide | To the Dog's Understanding

20

2

Training with Covert Control and Overt Positive Reinforcement

My training system has both formal and informal components. The formal component occurs in three 5-minute training sessions a day, in the morning, afternoon, and evening. The informal component occurs in how the dog is handled during the rest of the day. This chapter gives an overview of the principles and techniques that you will follow in both formal and informal training.

Covert Control and Overt Positive Reinforcement

THE FACTS ABOUT dogs that we looked at in Chapter 1 create a number of clear imperatives for dog training. The first is that we must be able to check the dog's behavior with minimal force and to do so without the dog realizing our involvement in delivering that check. Insofar as is possible, the dog's behavior should be "corrected" only by the environment, as the dog perceives it, and not by the trainer. What the dog discovers for itself in this way, especially as a seven- to eleven-week-old puppy, it will remember and practice for life.

With many other training methods, the trainer becomes a bringer of pain in the dog's eyes. Instead of that, we want the dog to make us the focus of all of its positive associations. This will dramatically enhance the effectiveness of training.

If we wish to curb or limit some of our dogs' natural behaviors, like stealing Thanksgiving dinner while we watch the big game on TV, we must hide our actions from them. The product of being too direct in our response to Grandma's roast turkey hitting the floor is that they will fear us, or merely wait until we cannot interfere with their appetite for home cooking.

If we can create an unpleasant experience for the dog when it first tries to steal food from the counter or the table, and it can only associate this experience with its own actions, it will never repeat the behavior, whether we are present or not. This is to everyone's advantage. We need never again worry about having to hide the tooth marks in the Thanksgiving turkey from our guests, especially that nosy Aunt Florence from Minneapolis (on your spouse's side of the family), and the dog is free from fear of punishment for doing what comes naturally.

We accomplish this with the aid of lines of different lengths that we attach to the dog's flat collar. We use an eight- to ten-foot line inside the house, and a thirty- to sixty-foot line outside the house. After a few days of having a line attached to his collar, the dog will forget it, along with the collar, and treat it as part of its own body. The dog should always wear one of these lines until it is fully trained, but you should not leave a long line on an unattended dog.

Greta is completely unaware of the line, eagerly anticipating being released to chase the ball.

The Dude is doing what comes naturally. Luckily, he is wearing his light line and I can interrupt his feast while reserving my hands for praise.

I will explain the lines and their use in detail in Chapter 5. But the general idea is that when the dog engages in an unwanted behavior, we can pop the line—that is, pull on it or hold it with just enough firmness to interrupt the behavior—without the dog seeing that we are doing so, or we can simply stand on it to restrict the dog's movement. This will allow us to control the dog's movement around the house and yard and in the park with other dogs, and to interrupt any unwanted behavior it may engage in. We will be able to do this from a distance and from behind the dog's back to prevent any negative association with us or our presence.

Covert control in action. Stepping on the line allows you to control your dog covertly.

For example, suppose I take a young puppy into my fenced back-yard and it tries to run off to chase a squirrel. This is a habit I must nip in the bud, if the dog is to be safe from running into traffic in pursuit of another squirrel at another time and place.

When the dog starts to run, I stand on the end of the line and turn my back. When I hear a "yip" and feel the pressure in the line under my feet as the dog hits the end of the rope with its own momentum, I keep my back turned for a count of "one, one thousand." This helps convince the bewildered dog that I cannot be responsible for what just happened to it.

And then I turn around, show the dog my empty hands, and say kindly, "What's the matter? What happened? Come here, little puppy." I crouch down to meet the puppy with pets, praise, and a treat, ensuring that the recall—the dog's return to the handler—is a happy one. I can see the puppy thinking, "Oh, Dale, you wouldn't believe it. The worst thing in the world happened. I'll never run away from you again."

If we need to use the line occasionally when the dog can see us, and we do so casually, it will take little notice. A good example of this is when the pup runs under the bed with a slipper. We can calmly and gently pull the dog out with the long line and then take away the slipper. We will thus be able to interrupt all the dog's unwanted behaviors unobtrusively.

We will always follow up such interruptions with a happy recall, even if it's only from a few inches away, to ensure that the dog feels most safe and well rewarded when it is near us. We will reserve our hands for praise and pets and never punish it or cause it discomfort while it is close to us. This will encourage the dog to trust us and prevent the breaking down of the bond that is at the heart of the relationship between us. We will never do anything that causes the dog to see us as bringers of pain.

To heighten the dog's sense that it is "free" when it is on a long line, we will use the leash attached to a flat collar, or if necessary to a Halti brand head collar, as a means of overt control on our daily walks (see Chapter 6 for more on walks and on the Halti head collar, including why its unique design makes it superior to all other head collars and harnesses on the market). But we will never cause the dog pain or discomfort in doing so. When we release the dog from the leash, it will believe itself to be "free," but in fact it will be on the long line and therefore still be under our control.

A dog trained in my method will willingly sit and wait for permission to go into the house.

This contrast will further serve the illusion that we are not participating in the dog's control when the leash is not in our hands, and therefore the limits we have put on its freedom will be even less visible to it. The dog will be happy to accept them as a natural part of life.

On the other side of things, we will always show the dog love and affection, and sometimes provide treats, when it pays attention to us or behaves in ways that please us. Every look in our direction will win positive reinforcement. Every look away will have uncertain, perhaps unpleasant consequences.

Throughout the early phases of training, I reserve my hands for praise and pleasure, using them only to give comfort and food, not discipline, and never even to move the dog into a desired position. For training to be effective, we cannot take what we want from the dog; the dog must give it willingly.

Covertly interrupting the dog when it engages in unwanted behaviors gradually builds a picture in the dog's mind, a world view, that chewing the furniture, soiling the rug, showing aggression to a person or another dog, chasing the neighbor's cat, and so on will naturally and inevitably backfire. If we are consistent, these associations will become part of the dog's belief system—its own internal set of rules—for life, and the dog will never connect them with a human agent. The dog that does not believe it can chase the cat, root in the trash, or take food from the table safely will refrain from these activities whether a human being is present or not.

Consistency is essential not only in interrupting unwanted behaviors but in all our practices throughout training. Consistency is the primary determiner of reliability in training. Failure to reinforce a rule even ten percent of the time produces no rule at all.

Teaching Behaviors
with Operant Conditioning

IN ADDITION TO creating a situation in which the dog's instinctual and habitual strategies fail it, we must create positive associations with the behaviors we do want. For this we begin with operant techniques. Taking a page from Pavlov, as Karen Pryor did, we teach the dog to associate a clicking sound—clickers designed for this purpose are commonly available at pet stores—with the provision of a food treat. Then we use the dog's own propensity to access reward to teach it to associate sitting, downing, standing, and coming to the trainer with the clicking and food treats. (For details on using the clicker, see Chapter 8.)

This stage of training is nonverbal. We deliberately avoid naming the desired behaviors because during this learning process we will see the worst responses from the dog. We want the dog's association to the words sit, stand, down, and so on to be the best responses it can give, when it is most confident and willing.

Besides this consideration, there is an even more important one in this stage of training: the need to establish benevolent eye contact with the dog. If you take from this book nothing but an understanding of how to build benevolent eye contact, you will be able to enhance your relationship with your dog dramatically.

Building Benevolent Eye Contact

AMONG DOGS, THE merest glance is full of meaning, and there is no behavior more significant than direct eye contact. When two dogs stare at one another, we know they will fight. And when we look directly at a dog, even our own dog, this represents a threat to it.

This is one of the reasons that dogs are so reluctant to come when called. It is also why children should learn not to stare at an aggressive or unfamiliar dog. There are unfortunately many similarities between canine threat and the way young children approach a dog, with their eyes wide, teeth showing in a smile that the dog sees as a preparation to bite, and arms waving about the head in the manner of striking a blow.

At the same time, the dog that will not look at your face is cut off from your subtlest, most meaningful body language and cannot obey you fully even if it wants to. Because the most powerful and the gentlest way to direct and hold the dog is with our eyes, we must begin by doing something that will diffuse and transform the psychological threat of eye contact, so that the dog may safely approach us even while we stare directly at it. The more dominant and confident the dog, the less difficulty we will have teaching this behavior; the more subordinate the dog, the harder we will have to work. In either case, we must remove the threat from direct eye contact.

Throughout operant conditioning with the clicker, we will gradually increase eye contact with the dog. Making comfortable eye contact with the dog will be necessary throughout all subsequent training. But even if you do no other training, benevolent eye contact will attune your dog to you strongly and dramatically increase its ability to cooperate with your wishes.

Chapter 7 explains how to build benevolent eye contact in detail. Let me now show you how covert control, clicker conditioning, and benevolent eye contact together advance training by describing one of my typical demonstrations for dog owners:

It's 10:00 AM Saturday morning. I walk into the conference room rented for today's seminar and look out at the participants. Fifteen dogs and their owners look back at me in anticipation. They are restless and moving about. Before this day is done, I will have to produce a down, recall, control, and benevolent eye contact with every dog here. I have never seen these dogs before, and they are of every breed and disposition, from large to small, from high to low drive, and from quiet and friendly to extremely aggressive.

I note immediately the large, assertive male in the front row. He is a crossbred dog, with Mastiff in his background. He must weigh at least 150 pounds. His owner casually leans back in his chair and barely bothers to hold the leash. Both dog and owner are happy with their position as "dominant pair" in the room. A young German Shepherd wanders a little too close, and in an instant the Mastiff is on his feet growling, tail straight up, staring the puppy down. The pup tucks his tail and heads for his owner's feet some ten feet away. The Mastiff glares around the room, daring anyone to approach.

"Keep your dogs close to you," I advise.

Down in the back is a young woman with a Pit Bull Terrier crossbreed who wouldn't mind a piece of action, but the owner has been wise enough to keep her dog well away from the others. Except now the Pit Bull has spotted a Jack Russell Terrier that looks like lunch and begins lunging toward it, roaring all the while. His feet tear at the floor, but he can gain no traction as he slips and slides about. The owner is struggling for control as the dog pulls heavily into the choke chain around his neck. I move quickly to the back of the room, Halti head collar in hand.

"Loosen the lead," I tell her.

"He'll go after him," she says, her face flushed with the effort to hold on.

"No, he won't," I reply. "He can't hear you while he's choking."

She loosens the lead, and the choker releases around the dog's neck. The Pit Bull immediately stops pulling.

"Call him to you," I tell her.

She calls the dog to her and he returns.

I approach, keeping my lead shoulder low and my posture loose and relaxed, and at the same time averting my face to avoid eye contact with the dog. He is not afraid of me, and if I pose no threat, he will be fine. I do not enter his critical zone, the five feet or so around him, but I stop at the edge and drop a piece of food. He wags his tail and walks up to me and sniffs the hot dog, then me. Then he eats the hot dog and wags his tail again. He bends his front legs slightly in a bowing gesture, asking for more. I am the holder of resources and therefore his superior. I feed him freely now, dropping the food at my feet, then direct my attention to the young woman.

I show the Halti to her and how it gently closes a dog's mouth. Then I carefully help her put it on the dog. I hand her a bag of food and instruct her to turn his head toward her, like using a halter on a horse, whenever he stares at another dog, then feed him when he looks at her. Ten minutes later the Pit Bull is asleep at her feet, dogs wandering all around him.

Back at the front of the room I notice a Collie crossbreed. He lies at his owner's feet, never moving. The owner is a large man, wearing a checkered shirt and a ball cap that says, "Fining Tractor." He looks me directly in the eye but does not smile. No, I say to myself, I don't suppose anybody argues with you. The Collie hides his head under a furry paw when he notices me looking at him.

With relative peace reigning in the room I give everyone an overview of good and bad training. By the time I've finished, the dogs are well socialized to the room, the owners are comfortable, and it's time to work the dogs. I cast my eye about the room. I want a neutral dog to begin the demo. I choose a young terrier that appears clever and full of fun.

I ask the owner to bring him forward to the open work area at the front of the room.

"Is there a specific problem?" I ask.

"He just doesn't pay attention to me," the owner replies.

I take the dog's leash off and exchange it for a long line, making sure the dog notices the removal of his leash. I make a dramatic gesture of throwing the leash on the floor nearby. The mischievous terrier immediately heads for the other dogs, looking for a little fun. I step on the line and stop him. He turns to look at me. I look away before he turns and act as if I am involved in something else. He attempts to take off again. I stop him again. This time, however, I click the clicker and drop a piece of food. He is curious and alert and notices the food fall to the floor. He trots forward to eat, then turns again to leave. I immediately click and drop a piece of food. He stops in his tracks and runs to the food and eats.

He looks up at me. I click immediately and drop more food. He looks up again, and again I click and drop food. He comes forward and eats. This time when he looks up, I drop my shoulder and look away. I begin to slowly move away from him. When he takes one step toward me, I click and drop food. Now he begins to follow me around while I click and drop food.

When it is clear that he understands that the sound of the reinforcer is a precursor to food, I turn directly and face him, a much more threatening behavior. I neither move nor speak. He stands and looks, then cocks his head sideways in puzzlement. I do nothing. Then thirty seconds later, he does what almost all pet dogs will do: he sits. I click and drop five pieces of food. He runs up and eats, then stands and stares, but this time only ten seconds elapse before he sits. Three more repetitions and he is sitting faster and more often than I can click and throw the food.

I have put the dog firmly in control of the situation, letting him decide the character of our interaction. Now I can extend his decision-making abilities, guiding him to choose to do what is in our mutual best interest.

He sits again expectantly. I do nothing. He gets up and whines, then sits again. This time I squat down and draw his nose to the ground using a piece of food as a lure. When his elbows hit the ground I click and drop a handful of food. Two minutes later he is downing over and over. Once again the behavior is coming almost more quickly than I can keep up. I walk away and he follows me wherever I go. He is ready for phase two.

I now go "cold" and stop the game. All the other dogs who are nearby are intrigued. They can smell and see the food and would like to participate. The terrier sits and downs in front of me, but I continue to ignore him. He sees the young Shepherd cross and takes off toward him. I step on the line and look away when he hits hard at the end. When he turns and looks at me, I display mock surprise at his dilemma and show him that my hands are empty and I have no leash.

I squat down and call him to me in a comforting tone. He runs over and stops, as most pet dogs do, about three feet away. I have food, but this time it's in my hand and he can't get to it unless he comes closer. I lure him in and feed him.

I get up, move away, and call him again, repeating this step until he runs to me on call and commits his body to mine, his chest touching my knee. Now that he is returning with confidence, I begin to raise his head with the food, forcing him to look me in the face to get the treat. The first time I do this, he backs up three feet, to the area where he feels safe, outside arm's length from the handler. But in a few repetitions he trusts me enough to come in close and briefly look me directly in the eye.

I go back to my conditioned reinforcer, clicking and providing a treat whenever the dog sits, downs, recalls, and gives me his total attention. I walk around the room with him, still without a leash. We walk past other dogs and people and weave in and out of the chairs, and he never takes his eyes off me or leaves my side. He is done, and his owner now understands what he is willing to do, if handled properly. She can't believe this is her dog. I give her a bag of food and a clicker and tell her to go to the back of the room and copy what I have done until the dog focuses on her the way he focused on me.

Now it is time for a bad boy. I pick the Mastiff at the front of the room. Operant conditioning will only make an aggressive or dominant dog worse if used improperly. Operant conditioning raises a dog's confidence, and this is not only unnecessary with dominant, aggressive dogs, but it can be counterproductive and dangerous. I will therefore limit the use of the clicker to making friends with this dog.

I ask the owner to hold onto the dog's leash while I socialize him. I notice he's wearing a "pinch" collar and tell the owner to switch over to a flat collar while I work. Pain from corrective collars is often interpreted as stimulation by aggressive dogs and serves to enrage them further.

I approach the Mastiff casually and look elsewhere as if I were merely walking by. I stop just outside the length of his leash and click the clicker, then drop food. I walk away only to find the dog right behind me. The owner has dropped the leash!

The Mastiff bangs me hard with his head, demanding food. I click and throw the food ten feet away. By the time he eats it and turns around, I have his leash in my hands. He knows what this means and he becomes a little more respectful. I click and reward him for a couple of minutes to ease the strain between us. I then put my long line on the dog as well. I ask the owner, "Has he shown aggression towards people?"

"Yes," he answers.

"Several times?"

"Yes."

"How about children?"

"Yes."

"He goes after the grandkids," his wife pipes in.

"Have you tried a Halti rather than the pinch collar?"

"Yes, but he fought it every day really hard, so I gave up," he replies.

"So you took the dog on and then let him win?"

"I suppose," he replies.

"I don't think you should own this dog," I say.

His wife smiles and looks at me. "Thank you," she says. I turn back to the man.

"It is not fair to the children around this dog to leave them vulnerable to attack. You cannot take on an aggressive dog and fail to win. You only succeed in empowering him further. This is a problem that must be handled by an expert, if it is to be solved at all. I will discuss this with you during the break, okay?"

"Okay."

I continue to work with the Mastiff. I show him a strong physical presence with no threat. I begin eye contact with my arm outstretched and my face turned away. I control the resources and stingily reward his half-hearted behaviors. In ten minutes he is following me like a puppy and doing downs, and staying down. He makes eye contact now with a pleading face. He paws the ground before me and half bows in a gesture of willingness. I give the dog back to the owner.

I turn my attention to the puppy at the feet of the "Fining Tractor" man. I approach very softly and ask, "What's the problem?"

"He doesn't listen, he runs away all the time, and he pees on the floor."

The pup is under the chair, trembling. He has been driven deep into defense and is showing avoidance and strong submission.

I make myself as small as possible by squatting down. I look away from the pup and click and drop food around me. He is hungry. He gets up and approaches, grabs some food, and runs back to safety. This is approach/avoidance behavior like that of squirrels in the park, whose desire for the offered peanut drives them forward until defense kicks in and causes a retreat, each attempt bringing them closer and closer, three steps forward, two steps backward, until they have the peanut. If you are patient enough, over time they will climb on you and take the nut from your pocket!

Eventually the pup is beside me, trying to make friends. I carefully guide him around to a position where my face is visible and attach a light line to control any retreat.

Feeling safe, the pup gets bolder and wants to make friends. With each piece of food I give him, I draw him more and more into looking at my face and eventually my eyes. I now lie face down on the floor and cover my head with my hands.

The pup delights in crawling on top of me and licking frantically at my ears. This is as nonthreatening a posture as I can show, and it quickly brings him out of his defensive behavior. I get up onto my knees and engage with him, drawing his face ever closer to mine, and deepening the eye contact. At the beginning, his eyes are mere slits, his ears pinned back on his head, and his face showing the tremendous stress involved. Slowly he lets down; his eyes round out and his ears lift off his head.

I get up and run away from him. He happily chases me, tail wagging. Now I make him commit to eye contact each time he approaches. I stand up and look at him, and he stands his ground. I begin to click and throw food. In five minutes I have a sit and a down, and a superb recall. I turn to his owner.

"He runs away because he is afraid," I say. "He is not 'peeing in your house,' he is submissively urinating in an attempt to neutralize the threat he feels."

The owner nods. "I've never seen him so happy," he says.

"Do you need him to work on the farm with you?" I ask.

"No, we're not running the farm anymore," he replies.

"I bet you had some pretty tough dogs around in those days."

"Yes!" he says, with a smile of appreciation for my understanding.

"Use a soft voice to speak to him and gentle corrections. He is a sensitive pup and doesn't need so firm a hand."

"Okay, good. I understand," he says.

"Very nice dog," I say to him. "Do lots of eye contact and the urination will stop. He wants to please you; he is just soft."

I hand the puppy back to the owner and take a deep breath and look out into the room. It's going to be a great day.

In the course of a demonstration, I know that sooner or later I will hear five comments from dog owners: (1) "You didn't tell the dogs to do anything"; (2) "You never touched the dogs except to pet them when they came to you"; (3) "Every dog reacted differently, but they all wound up doing exactly what you wanted"; (4) "You give the dogs so much food"; and (5) "Once you began working with my dog, it forgot all about me."

To follow my system, you do not tell the dog what to do and do not touch except to pet in the early stages of training, because it is essential that the dog decide for itself what to do. The whole notion of giving a dog commands is misguided. A human being can follow a command perfectly without question. A dog can only respond, positively or negatively, to a signal with which it has positive or negative associations.

The third typical comment touches on another crucial aspect of good training: There is a schedule for training, but there is no schedule for results. One dog may take three weeks or even three months to learn what another dog learns perfectly in three days. Often, the smarter the dog, the longer the training that is required. A clever dog, like a clever child, has more things going on in its conscious mind and is quicker to see opportunities for mischief.

In my system, training proceeds at the dog's individual pace. A stage of training is complete when it is complete to the dog's understanding, not a moment before. You know the dog's understanding is complete when you see that it knows how to escape confusion and discomfort—here the discomfort is simply the lack of food reward—by offering a behavior that you have taught it to associate with positive reinforcement.

Another hallmark of my training is the plentiful use of food in the early stages. Some trainers speak dismissively of "bribing" the dog with food. The key is to use the food as a reinforcement for success and then gradually make the food treats less frequent. If this is done properly, the dog will give desired behaviors more and more purely on signal, with no more reward than an occasional "good dog" and a kindly look in the eye, because of the positive associations it has formed with those behaviors. I do not believe there is an effective way to train an animal without food treats, however.

Then there's that fifth comment: "My dog forgot all about me." The trainer who uses my methods becomes the benevolent center of all the dog's positive experiences. If you follow them, that will happen for you, too. Perhaps the greatest benefit of my methods is how they foster your dog's increasingly positive focus on, and responsiveness to, you.

Compassionate Compulsion:
Using the Bench

AS TRAINING ADVANCES, it is necessary to use some form of compulsion, or force, to achieve full reliability. Trainers who claim that reliability can be achieved without any compulsion are either trying to pull the wool over your eyes or unwittingly sharing their own self-delusion about dogs. All guide dog organizations employ compulsion in training because it is the only way they can ensure that the dog will serve its owner reliably. What we want, then, is a means of compassionate compulsion that will never hurt the dog.

The problems that accompany the application of force to a dog are many and varied. One thing is certain: These problems are extremely destructive to the bond that is at the heart of why we keep dogs, and why they "keep" us! The end result of applying force is often worse than the problem that brought about its use in the first place. You cannot apply force to a dog without producing negative consequences. All good trainers know this and make allowance for this reality.

If we are going to apply pressure to a dog, it must know how to escape it. But the dog must never escape through submission, avoidance, or aggression, even though these are the tools Mother Nature has provided for this purpose. The dog must learn to escape through compliance. In other words, when the dog feels pressure, it must learn to escape that pressure by giving a trained behavior or response, as opposed to trying to escape from the influence of the owner by running away, lying on its back, or acting aggressively, for example.

It is important to understand that touching a dog to direct or guide it in any way, no matter how gently, is compulsion. It may not be a very strong form of compulsion, but it is compulsion none the less! As Chapter 1 explained, force may seem to work, in that it makes the dog sit, for example, but over time force inevitably produces resentment at the least and defense at the worst. This is why so many young dogs do well in group obedience classes at six months old and become unmanageable pests at one year old. If I had a dollar for every time I've heard clients say, "She was such a good little dog; she was the best in her class at obedience school. Now she's a terror and won't listen to us at all," I'd be a rich man.

If we hope to achieve the best results between human and dog, we must never do anything that causes the dog to fear or resent us, no matter how well it seems to work at the time. We therefore need a method that will allow us to apply pressure to the dog but avoid the negative consequences that accompany the use of force. This method is climbing the dog onto a small bench, where its mobility is restricted.

The bench will help us show the dog in very clear terms what it must do to escape from compulsion—always by acting in its own best interests to the best of its understanding. The bench will allow us to present the solution to this problem in terms the dog can readily and easily understand. Through the proper use of the bench, we will take away and ultimately cause the dog to abandon its greatest advantage over us: its superior speed and mobility.

Just how slow and clumsy we are in comparison to them is something all too many dogs learn as puppies and then use to escape our control for the rest of their lives. There is no situation more instructive in this regard than going to the park and watching a frustrated owner call his dog, then yell at his dog, and then chase his dog, lunging out for the dog with his hands at every opportunity while Fluffy tears around him staying just out of reach! This is a behavior that would never even occur to a properly bench-trained dog.

I use a bench of the kind available in most garden stores, something about two feet high with a rectangular surface roughly twenty-two by twenty-four inches, just large enough for the dog to stand, sit, and lie down on it. For small dogs, a smaller bench will do.

In training dogs on the bench, we take away their mobility in a way that is physically painless. Insofar as the dog finds the bench psychologically uncomfortable at first, we dissipate the discomfort with benevolent eye contact and food treats.

Bench training, which is designed to show the dog how to escape compulsion into a positively reinforced behavior, starts after benevolent eye contact is well established. Up to this point, we have reserved our hands for petting and comforting only. Bench training includes the first use of the hands on the dog for something besides petting, such as gradually increasing pressure on a leash attached to a flat collar or touching the dog to guide it into position. Gentle though these techniques are, the dog still experiences them as compulsive force, and that is an experience we always want to minimize.

Many other training systems use compulsion, usually in the form of a choke chain, without ever showing the dog how to escape into compliance. My training system uses compulsion, in the form of having the dog climb up onto a bench into a space of restricted mobility, only after teaching the dog how to cope with the accompanying stress and then escape compulsion into positively rewarded compliance. And in my method, the hands are never used to discipline the dog.

In a nutshell, a combination of operant conditioning and benevolent eye contact off the bench teaches the dog what it should do and prepares it to learn the escape when we move to the bench. It does what it should do reliably on signal on or off the leash and for anyone, even a child, because of the training on the bench. (For detailed instructions on using the bench, see Chapters 10 and 11.)

Clicker Conditioning and Dominant Dogs

THERE IS ONE exception to the sequence of building benevolent eye contact, clicker training, and bench work. Although all animals learn through engaging in successful and unsuccessful behaviors, the basis of operant conditioning, not all dogs will respond appropriately to the clicker.

Just as classical conditioning with a choke chain and leash can have unwanted and unpredictable side effects, so can operant conditioning. Operant conditioning emboldens the dog, and there is little good to be had in emboldening the already bold dog. A perfectly reasonable puppy can be changed into a totally unreasonable dog by the use of operant conditioning. Dogs that are not driven by food or are dominant aggressive, systems wise (a dog that fails to respond appropriately because it anticipates and/or avoids negative outcomes in whatever training system is being used and resents and resists being manipulated in this way), or sharp shy (see Chapters 3 and 17 for a discussion of dog types and temperaments) can be inappropriate subjects for the clicker. If your dog fits one of these descriptions, you can skip the clicker stage and go right to the bench once you have established benevolent eye contact.

WITH THIS OVERVIEW of how to train, let's consider the all-important question of choosing the right dog to train, by which I mean, the right dog for you.

3

Choosing the Right Dog

Of the many pitfalls that stand between a dog owner and peaceful contentment, owning the "wrong dog" is the least understood and the most difficult to overcome. All dogs are born with both defense and prey drives, for example, but right off the bat some dogs are primarily defense dogs, while others are primarily prey dogs, and the variety spreads out from there. From this point of view, the object of training, for pet dogs as well as working dogs, is to bring the dog into balance with prey and defense. Using a prey dog tactic on a defense dog can be disastrous. For example, with the wrong training tactic, a dog may not be able to come on recall because of its approach/avoidance instincts. This puts the dog into a conflict it cannot resolve.

Disinformation from some dog organizations does little to help the situation. As much as it is implied that anyone can own any breed, this is not necessarily true. Dogs are not all the same, and the problem is not always with the owner. Pit Bulls are not necessarily sweet, loving dogs in the hands of everyone, let alone those who make this claim. Although they can at times appear to be, appearances can be deceiving.

Breeds differ for very important reasons. A dog meant to retrieve birds is going to have a very different disposition from one that is bred to fight to the death.

There are exceptions to every rule, but exceptions do not make the argument true. For example, I've been told, "I've owned Pit Bulls all my life, and I have never been hurt by one." Well, great. Unfortunately, this does not mean that the rest of us could do the same.

Another good example was when the TV show *Frasier* was popular. There was a Jack Russell Terrier in it, a very nice, but high-drive and aggressive breed of dog. This caused a run on Jack Russells at the breeders. It also produced a run on training for Jack Russells. The dog looked cute and manageable on TV (in the hands of an expert trainer), but Jack Russells are "ratters," vermin dogs that will go to ground to kill. They have larger incisors than a German Shepherd and are willing to use them. They are tough as nails, as they should be, given the purpose for which they were bred.

The honest breeders warned people and tried to make sure that buyers understood what they were getting into, but few people listened. There were some tragic results and a lot of unhappiness until the interest in this breed slowed down. If we are going to own dogs that possess special skills or are driven to particular behaviors by their genetics, we need to acquire special skills in order to handle them. The Jack Russell Terrier is a good pet for the right owners, but the reality of the dog is not what was shown on the TV show *Frasier*. The same cautions apply to many other breeds that become fashionable for one reason or another.

In the modern world, far removed from any working knowledge of dogs, people tend to buy dogs spontaneously, for emotional reasons. We buy dogs because they are cute or attractive to us or because we imagine that this breed or that will serve as good companions. Unfortunately, imagination founded on ignorance and whether a dog is cute or not are poor indicators of what it will be like to live with. Let's take a look at dogs and see what information we might find and turn to our advantage in choosing one to own.

Dog Groups and Breeds

DOGS ARE DIVIDED first into seven groups, and every group is divided into many breeds (see "The Seven Groups of Dogs" later in this chapter). The American Kennel Club (AKC) and the Canadian Kennel Club (CKC) both recognize some 150 breeds, and there is good reason for this variety. Almost every breed in the world at some time or another served a working purpose, and some still do. From the ratters and other vermin-hunting dogs to the hounds, herders, retrievers, and protectors, we altered the dog to serve us.

A particular dog looks and acts the way it does for a reason. You may have noticed how the herding dogs tend to move in wide circles, the terriers dig, the hounds bay and howl, and the protectors bark and threaten. This does not happen by accident; these are genetic predispositions that are deliberately bred into the dog, along with length of fur, color, height and weight, shape of head, depth of muzzle, length of neck, placement of eye and ear, and so on.

As the Germans say, "The German Shepherd who will not protect his master is not a German Shepherd." As the hunters say, "The retriever who will not retrieve isn't worth anything." We must expect that particular behaviors will be part of the breed we own. Some dogs are meant to bite and some are not. When was the last time you heard of a pack of Irish Setters attacking anyone? Never!

But we hear almost daily of attacks by Pit Bulls, Rottweilers, Dobermans, and German Shepherds, among others. This is not just about bad owners, as some would like to claim; it's also about breed type. If you buy a dog from a breed that has a history of aggression, you should expect to see aggression and train to control it. By the same token, if you buy a Golden Retriever and it starts biting everyone, something is wrong!

Properly bred dogs should, and for the most part do, behave in predictable ways. This is the whole point in having breeds in the first place.

Who Are You?

THIS QUESTION IS not only the title of a great song by the Who. It's also an important question to ask yourself before you choose a dog.

People, like dogs, come in differing shapes, sizes, and dispositions. If you are quiet and retiring in nature, and your children are the same, get a female from a smaller-sized, easy-going breed. If your kids play football and love to be rough-and-tumble and you like to run after work and play pickup baseball on weekends, get a male from a larger, more outgoing breed from the Sporting or Herding groups. If you are a couch potato and activity to you means operating the remote control to the TV, don't get a German Shepherd.

If you want protection as well as companionship, the police will tell you without hesitation that the best deterrent to being broken into or attacked is a dog. Many of the criminal incidents, such as home invasions, that are reported in the media would never have happened if the victim had owned a dog with the right instincts. I certainly feel a lot better at night when I'm traveling away from home knowing that no one in their right mind is going to try to get near my family or get into my house, thanks to my import German Shepherd bitch.

But you must be realistic about owning such a dog. The police will also tell you without hesitation that protection dogs are a responsibility to own. They must be fully trained, properly contained in a secure manner, and under control at all times.

Children and other people have a right to be safe from your dog. You cannot buy a working dog, not train it, and then say you didn't know it would hurt anyone when it bites to protect you. You cannot blame the breeder for producing aggressive dogs when that's what the dog's purpose is. But we can blame breed organizations that are not forthcoming about the nature of dogs and dog breeds.

Ill-informed enthusiasts for certain breeds often argue that all dogs, of whatever breed, will bite. To say this, and no more, is to ignore the huge disparities in the odds that dogs of different breeds will bite a person. It is an outright lie to claim that the likelihood of biting is not also a product of breed behavior. Some dogs are far more genetically likely to bite than others, not just because their owners "made them mean" but because their breeding made them predisposed to bite.

Not all dogs are created equal and not all dogs are meant to be happy, loving companions either. You have a responsibility to yourself and your family, and to the dog, to choose well and be honest with yourself about your intentions and willingness to train.

Show Lines and Working Lines

MANY BREEDS OF dogs are bred both for show and for work. This means that in selecting breeders, it is important to know whether they are breeding their dogs primarily for appearance or for the dog's traditional function.

The show game is essentially a beauty pageant. Generally, dogs bred for show purposes are selected for their appearance more than their behavior, because they will be judged not on how they behave but on how they look. These dogs spend most of their "working" lives sitting in crates waiting for their five minutes in the show ring under the judge's eye. A dog that cannot sit or lie calmly for hours at a time waiting for its turn in the ring will not make a good show prospect.

This is not to say that all show dogs will be calm and easy to handle, but they have not been selected for their high drive levels or the expectation that they will run all day long retrieving birds or herding sheep. For this reason, show dogs can be preferable as pets when lower activity levels are required.

Working dogs are bred for just that: work. They are selected for their high drive levels and natural inclination to a task. They are not selected for their looks, and working dogs of the same breed can differ broadly in appearance. They must possess the intelligence necessary to accomplish the work that is expected of them. They are often hardy and tough, willful, driven, and strong. They tend to be healthier and smarter, though not always, and a heck of a lot harder to handle.

If you have an active lifestyle that includes things like running, riding horses, and hiking on weekends, this is the choice for you. At the same time, I have seen many failures that can be attributed to the working-style dog just being too much dog for the average owner.

Information on show-bred dogs can be found by accessing the AKC Web site (see the Resources section at the end of the book). Information on working dogs is available through hunting clubs, retrieving clubs, gun and shooting magazines, and specialty clubs like Schutzhund USA. As a final point on this subject, there are some breeders who produce show dogs that will work, and vice versa; however, these breeders are the exception rather than the rule.

A Closer Look at the Groups

WE CAN GAIN valuable information from the seven groups that dogs are divided into by the AKC. These are the Sporting, Hound, Working, Terrier, Toy, Non-Sporting, and Herding dogs. The AKC breed standards give a brief description of each dog and some history and background on the animal.

The Seven Groups Of Dogs

THE AKC, CKC, and other major kennel clubs commonly divide dogs into seven groups:

HERDING GROUP. Dogs such as the Border Collie, Corgi, and German Shepherd

WORKING GROUP. Dogs such as the Great Dane, Rottweiler, and Saint Bernard

SPORTING GROUP. Dogs such as the English Cocker Spaniel, the Labrador Retriever, the Golden Retriever, and the Weimaraner

NON-SPORTING GROUP. Dogs such as the Bull Dog, the Lhasa Apso, and the Schipperke

HOUND GROUP. Dogs such as the Dachshund, the Irish Wolfhound, and the Rhodesian Ridgeback

TERRIER GROUP. Dogs such as the American Staffordshire Terrier, the Border Terrier, and the Irish, Scottish, and Welsh Terriers

TOY GROUP. Dogs such as the Cavalier King Charles Spaniel, the Chihuahua, and the Pomeranian

You can find information on the different groups and all the different breeds in books and from interest groups and Web sites devoted to dogs in general or to specific breeds. See the Resources section at the end of the book for good places to start.

Dogs within the same group may have been bred for different purposes, and this is another issue to consider in choosing a breed. Let's look at the drafting, or pulling, dogs, the Husky-style dogs. These dogs need to understand four tasks to be successful: "Go," "Stop," "Right," and "Left." This represents a very simple interaction between man and dog. The dog must be powerful and determined. It does not need to be intelligent, considerate of people, or particularly obedient.

Accordingly, if we get one of these dogs, we can expect an animal that is difficult to train, stubborn, willful, aggressive, and independent. It solves problems by overpowering them. Social disputes are solved by fighting. Such an animal will be "fundamental" in its behavior, as there is no need for wits when pulling a load all day.

All breeds respond to positive training methods. Even the hearty and independent Bloodhound willingly works.

The indigenous peoples of the world and others who have traditionally employed dogs for pulling work have usually done so with a whip in hand. This is not because they have been cruel but because the whip has been a necessary tool for the situation. It serves, in effect, as a conditioned reinforcer. Once a dog has felt the whip, the mere cracking sound of it will go a long way to keeping the dog focused on pulling the sled rather than mauling its teammate.

Sled dogs will also be a grooming nightmare because they carry a heavy coat to meet the conditions under which they have worked for many generations. They are attractive, to be sure. But are you really ready for such a dog?

Or let's consider the hounds. Historically, hounds required no commands whatsoever. They have been used since ancient times to hunt in packs. Their purpose is to hunt down and kill or disable game. No human direction can micromanage this most natural of dog behaviors. One can notice the use of whips in managing packs of hounds to this day.

Hounds also settle social differences by fighting. They come in all sizes and shapes, but their purpose is to kill and maim. An animal that will engage in a fight to the death with everything from a rat to a lion gains no survival advantage by listening to us!

My family has a Miniature Wire-Haired Dachshund named Dewey, also known as Dude in honor of the Jeff Bridges character in the Coen Brothers' movie, *The Big Lebowski*. The Dude is a great dog, loyal and loving. He is also stubborn, independent, unforgiving, and tough as nails. At all of ten pounds, he is more aggressive than our German Shepherd and a fearsome defender. He is a handful to own and manage. I personally wouldn't want to see this disposition in a dog that weighs eighty pounds or more!

The result of honest and fair training is total trust. Here the rough-and-tumble Duck Tolling Retriever, Rhime, gives me a kiss.

This brings me to the Rhodesian Ridgeback, a dog bred to hunt lions in Africa. I love "Ridgies" and have trained several for clients. They are loyal, clever, and trainable (as are almost all dogs), but you have to know what you are doing and accept what you are getting into when you buy such a dog. Are you ready for that?

On the other hand, the retrieving dogs—Golden Retrievers, Labs, and so forth—are very used to control and to heeding multiple commands. They have a totally modified hunting drive, so that they will only retrieve, not kill or harm. Thanks to a long history of cooperation with human beings and careful breeding, they are pliable, obedient, and responsive, they listen well, and they have low aggression levels.

Together with dogs from the Sporting group, dogs from the Herding group have the longest genetic history of listening to and cooperating with human beings. They display self-control, accept leadership, will defer to people, and are modified hunters that will not harm the livestock. They are very intelligent, social, disposed to obey lots of signals, and easy to train. Herding dogs do tend to have more aggression bred into them than sporting dogs, however, because they need it for the tough work of keeping cattle and other animals in line as well as fighting off predators.

The herding dogs are among my favorites. Here's Penny showing off with a perfect "stand."

With the wide variety of dog breeds available, you must take an honest look at yourself and your family, and just as you would with purchasing a car or van, you must take the time to research the whole idea of owning a dog. Weigh your lifestyle, activity level, and wants and needs. Ask people you know about their dogs, chat with dog owners in the park or on walks, and contact organizations like the AKC and CKC and the various breed clubs to get information on breeders of the dogs that interest you. Then visit the best breeders in your area and talk with them. They are the experts in the health and behavior of their own dogs. Breeders are not always forthcoming or honest, but the good ones are, and they will help you to choose correctly because they want the best for their puppies.

Choosing a Puppy

BECAUSE OF THE dog's special developmental schedule, it is always best to begin your relationship with a dog as a puppy. If you get a dog when it is seven to eight weeks old, you have an irreplaceable opportunity to begin training the dog when it does by far its best learning. This time in the puppy's life is called the *imprinting period* and lasts from approximately seven to eleven weeks of age. What a dog learns in those weeks stays with it for the rest of its life.

This does not mean that you cannot train an older puppy well. As I mentioned in Chapter 1, any dog under three years old is still a puppy, and throughout this book I use the words pup, puppy, and dog interchangeably, except where I refer specifically to older dogs.

When choosing a puppy for a pet, look for the golden middle. You do not want the pup that is too bold and in your face all the time. But even more important, you must never choose the shy, frightened pup, no matter how much your heart goes out to it. This pup is nothing but trouble and heartbreak for all concerned. (For more on dogs with extreme temperaments or behavioral profiles, see "The Shelter Dog," coming up in the chapter, and Chapter 16, "Difficult Dogs.")

Choose the pup that is happy to come and play with you but is also content sniffing around on its own or playing with its littermates. It should go back and forth between these behaviors and generally show an easygoing disposition. It must never show fear, and it should be willing to go for a little walk with you (with the breeder's permission), and be happy and confident while seeing new things.

The Older Dog

PERHAPS YOU HAVE a grown dog that you'd now like to train and you're wondering if old dogs can really learn new tricks. Indeed, they can.

Older dogs are often resistant to change because of their previous experiences. They have abandoned the pleasures of puppyhood and all the good things that come with it. Puppies are easier to train than older dogs, precisely because they are more eager to play. As we'll see in later chapters, play opens the door to the most effective methods of teaching and highest rates of retention during the learning process.

For this reason, when an older dog is brought to me because of a behavior problem, I often try to cajole it into puppylike play. I play and goof around, and will get down on my hands and knees to tickle and romp with even the oldest, most withdrawn dog. This sometimes draws remarks from passersby who catch me in my sillier moments. My goofiness may also startle the dog, because older dogs have frequently become accustomed to being treated with indifference. In fact, behavior problems in older dogs mostly arise because their owners have stopped paying positive attention to them. Negative attention from the owner is better than no attention, and so a dynamic of bad behavior begins to establish itself in the dog.

A playful, happy dog, whatever its age, is a quick study in a game involving learning something new. The easygoing and relaxed attitude of play opens the mind and allows the muscles, long stressed with tension, to let down and release. And it is immensely rewarding for the trainer when serious older dogs begin to play as they did when they were puppies.

No dog is too old to play. And no person is, either. Show the older dog that you are fun to be with. Remind the dog of the happier times of its youth and you will both be the better for it. If you acquire an older dog that needs training, your first training sessions should simply be play sessions. When you see the dog becoming comfortable in its play with you, you can commence training in earnest.

The Shelter Dog

THE IDEA OF rescuing an unwanted animal can be very attractive, not to mention the high prices that many good breeders charge for their dogs. But animals that have wound up in the pound or shelter, often through no fault of their own, have also usually suffered seriously before being placed there. That means they will need special care and training.

As much as our hearts go out to them, shelter dogs are where they are because they have failed to live up to the expectations of at least one owner, and sometimes several owners, before arriving at their destination. I like to think that even the worst owners have tried hard, in their limited way, to give these dogs a home. Many of these dogs have repeatedly bitten, barked, and destroyed their way into the situation in which they now find themselves. Even in cases where the dog is far more sinned against than sinning, and even in cases of very young dogs, an animal's presence in the shelter likely indicates a traumatic past that will cause problems in the future.

Shelters have the best intentions, and shelters successfully adopt out good dogs every day. But so many dogs and other animals are abandoned to their care that even the best-run shelters can be overwhelmed; as a result, they are not equipped to assess and remediate every animal's individual problems. For example, some shelter dogs have hidden triggers for aggression, which is to say that because of their prior experiences, they have formed associations to human behaviors that may appear innocuous to us but cause them to bite in self-defense. There is no way to predict these events, because the triggers can be as simple as petting the dog in an "incorrect" manner. There may be no opportunity for a shelter to discover that a dog has such a hidden trigger for aggression.

The result is that time and time again, the wrong dogs are inadvertently placed with the wrong people. And dogs that no average pet owner should be expected to handle are placed in improper homes.

Because good dogs can be adopted from shelters, but because this will inevitably be much riskier than obtaining a dog from a good breeder, I recommend that only experienced dog people look for a dog at a shelter. Single people, couples without children, semiretired and retired people, and those who work at home—if they have sufficient experience with dogs—can all benefit from, and bring benefit to, unwanted dogs in need of a home.

However, I strongly advise families with children to find a reputable breeder and buy a purebred puppy. You are going to own this animal for at least ten years. You and your kids and the dog deserve the best chance you can get at success. Taking someone else's mistakes into your home represents a poor way to start.

In many ways the odds are stacked against both shelter operators and prospective dog owners. Dogs are perfectly capable of hiding behaviors when it suits them to do so, or again, the shelter environment may simply not trigger any problematical behavior. The shelter environment can also intimidate dogs and suppress their problematical behaviors, until the environment changes and allows the behaviors to reemerge as the dog regains confidence.

Because of this reality, I can only offer the following advice for choosing a dog at a shelter. You must let reason be your guide and not bite off more than you can chew. Your well-being and the safety of others around you depend on the decision you make when getting a dog. Rescuing a dog is no good if it ends tragically.

For those with the time, patience, energy, and experience with dogs to try owning a shelter dog, there are some important issues to consider. First, let's acknowledge once more that shelters contain perfectly good dogs that are there for no fault of their own. These exceptions do not invalidate the rule or represent a sound argument for adopting.

Remember that a dog imprints between seven and eleven weeks of age, which means that its character and habits are permanently formed at the end of this period. Even in the best of circumstances, shelter dogs will usually require a greater effort to accomplish less in every aspect and stage of training, both because they are almost always a good deal older than eleven weeks of age and because of their prior experiences.

Even if the puppies have been born in the shelter and are still in their imprinting period, the unfortunate fact is that they cannot escape being affected by the distress of their mothers and the other animals in the shelter. By the time these puppies are seven or eight weeks old and are ready to be adopted out, they may already be traumatized in ways that are almost impossible to remediate.

Depending on their background and the length of time dogs have been at the shelter, it may be impossible to house-train them. Having grown up with little if any correct stimulation, they have often learned to resort to chewing, digging, and barking to amuse themselves. These are firmly embedded habits that can border on the impossible to change. Some of these dogs may also have developed the habit of escaping containment and wandering about in search of food and recreation, much to the dismay of the previous owners' neighbors. This is not to mention that they can be extremely dog aggressive, people aggressive, and child aggressive, depending on their background.

The correct method for dealing with dogs adopted from shelters is to take complete control of their lives. During the initial phases of rehabilitation especially, the dog should be watched carefully whenever it is out of its crate (for information on the crate's role in training, see Chapter 5). The long line will be an invaluable tool for reshaping the dog's view of the world (for the general principle of the long lines, see Chapter 2; for specific examples of how to use them, see Chapter 5). There must be no freedom for this dog whatsoever. Do not give the shelter dog the chance to screw up its life once again. Take control.

On the other hand, give the dog plenty of affection and positive reinforcement. If the dog likes to fetch, play the game often (see Chapter

5 for how to teach the fetch). Be liberal with treats and pets, and keep the dog close to you at all times. Build up the bond between the two of you through benevolent eye contact (see Chapter 7), so that the dog learns to trust and depend upon you. And then begin training as described in this book.

Breed Rescue Groups

BREED RESCUE GROUPS are able to screen their rescued dogs more closely than shelters usually can, and so offer a better chance of finding an appropriate dog. They have specific knowledge and information because of their expertise in dealing only with one breed.

Again, however, I recommend that only someone with sufficient time, patience, energy, and experience with dogs should seek a dog from a breed rescue organization. Dogs from breed rescue organizations may also have been traumatized by their earlier experiences and have hidden triggers for aggression or other problems.

This also applies to puppies born in a rescue situation. Although the chance of getting a good puppy from a breed rescue is greater than from a shelter, the experience of being born to a frightened, anxious mother has a powerful impact, which may be mediated by a change in hormone levels in the mother's milk. The strength of the bond between mother and offspring means that a puppy's first experiences will have long-lasting effects for good or ill, depending on the circumstances. As I mentioned earlier, I therefore recommend that families with children get a dog from a reputable breeder.

The possibility of hidden triggers for behavioral problems means that, as with shelter dogs, you must let reason be your guide in choosing a dog from a breed rescue group. Breed rescue volunteers may have no problems with a dog, because of their familiarity with their favorite breed and dogs in general. In less expert hands, problems may emerge with a vengeance.

There are good dogs to be found through breed rescues, nonetheless. If you have the experience and time to handle training such a dog, follow the procedure for shelter dogs above.

Your first goal with a dog from a shelter or a breed rescue group is to get the dog back to neutral, after the stress it has experienced before finding a home with you. Look for signs of stress—narrowed eyes, flattened ears, lowered tail, or raised hackles (hair standing up on the back of the neck and shoulders)—around daily activities, and give the dog time to accept its new environment.

Remember that benevolent eye contact is your best friend in this situation. It is a very powerful tool for lowering defense responses and fear in general. Go slowly and carefully in the beginning with all dogs, but be particularly cautious with the older dog. When the dog is no longer displaying fearful, anxious, or aggressive behaviors and body language, you can begin formal training.

You've Chosen a Dog, What's Next?

CHOOSING A DOG is a momentous decision. But before we discuss how to make the dog comfortable in its new home with you, let's consider some nuances of canine learning and dog–person communication that can have a profound impact on training.

Low-Stress,
High-Result Learning

As we saw in Chapter 1, dogs communicate with each other in complex ways, not through speech, but through their highly developed observational and gestural skills. Dogs write their *War and Peace* with the flick of a tail here and the twitch of an ear there, calibrating and managing every nuance of social hierarchy and every move in the hunt for resources in the wild.

Likewise, dogs watch us human beings carefully. Their success in reading our intentions and inclinations has enabled them to enter into our homes, and more important, into our hearts. But communication is supposed to be a two-way street, and we have lost the old stockmen's and farming families' ability to read what dogs try to tell us. What we are missing in consequence is information about the clarity, or lack thereof, of the dogs' understanding of what we want them to do, and about their confidence that they will be safe with us while they figure out the solution. In a word, we miss crucial information about how much stress a dog is experiencing.

All learning is physiologically and psychologically stressful to some extent. With heightened concentration, for example, blood pressure increases. Some stress is unavoidable. But as studies of dogs, dolphins, chimpanzees, parrots, and human beings have shown, the best and fastest learning occurs when there is the least consciously felt stress.

If we want training to succeed, we must recognize that the more stress a dog feels, the harder it will be for that dog to learn. This interference with the learning process leads to frustration for both the trainer and the dog.

Suppose someone asked you to repeat a complicated series of letters, words, and numbers that you had just been taught. Now imagine that the person yelled at you, acted in a threatening way, and even hit you while you tried to answer. You would be thinking more about the threat posed by the behavior of the questioner than the answer to the question! That is what classical conditioning with choke chains or pinch collars does to dogs, and it is counterproductive to all good training.

We do not do ourselves or the dog any service when we add stress to the learning situation. Stay calm and positive and use the right training techniques, however, and the results will speak for themselves. The first and most important step to limiting a dog's stress is paying attention to its mood.

Mood and Its Meaning in Training

JUST AS SURELY as environment creates behavior, mood drives behavior. Mood is powerfully tied to events by association, as is demonstrated by our response to a favorite song from the past, and through that memory, to the events of a specific time and place. The Canadian Oxford Dictionary defines mood this way.

> Mood: (1) a state of mind or feeling; (2) a fit of melancholy or bad temper; (3) inducing a particular mood; (4) the atmosphere or prevailing tone of a place, event, composition etc.; (5) "in the mood" or "in no mood": inclined or disinclined ("was in no mood to go dancing").

We all have experience with mood and its effects, whether in someone else or in ourselves. We all remember times when we wanted to do something and knew that if one of our parents was "in a bad mood," it was probably better to ask the other parent for permission. We have all had experiences with a boss at work who because of some circumstance beyond our control showed a change in behavior, and following that, a change in mood. What might normally have been a mild reprimand over some detail at work turned instead into a "talking to" in his office.

As the dictionary definition suggests, when we are in the mood to dance, we have endless energy and excitement about doing so. When we are not in the mood to dance, our efforts will be less than enthusiastic, or we may make no effort at all.

Moods attach strongly to particular behaviors, and engaging in the behavior triggers the mood. If, for example, we do something we enjoy, our mood becomes more positive and we feel happy and enthusiastic. When doing something we don't like, our mood may turn sullen. I particularly remember having to do the chore of washing dishes with my brother when I was growing up. We might have been getting along famously before this chore began, but a few minutes into the job, storm clouds would appear on the horizon and a bickering match, or even a fight, might soon follow.

We can see that circumstances will create a behavior, and mood will give the behavior its intensity. What is important to understand is that the behavior comes first and is followed by the feeling. These two experiences are attached by association.

In the dog, this is particularly so. If the dog's mood is not in keeping with the behavior we seek, the behavior will not have much intensity. This is why I stress so often that your behavior must be positive and encouraging during training, and that you must watch the mood of the dog carefully while you work.

Let's say, for example, that while you are teaching the dog the down, you are particularly frustrated by the dog's responses and begin to be a bit rough with the dog in an attempt to get it to comply. Or perhaps you are simply using forceful methods, because that is how you have been taught to train. During the process you pull harder and harder on the leash, while your voice rises in intensity and pitch as your emotions come to the surface.

An important thing to recognize right away is that the dog's resistance is being made part of its learning process. Meanwhile the dog's mood is being shaped by this negative experience, and the whole process is forming an association in the dog's mind between its mood and the trained behavior. When you polish off this brutal wrestling match by rewarding the dog for finally going down, you are also rewarding the dog for its resistance and attaching its "bad" mood permanently in a negative association to the down.

Every time you ask for the down from now on, the dog's association will be to the negative experience. The word alone will create the mood that the dog was in while it was being taught. This is why you so often see dogs going down slowly and reluctantly when "commanded" to do so after a course of classical conditioning with a choke chain or pinch collar.

Mood is created by all the associations that the dog makes during the process of learning. These associations—to time and place and the disposition of the trainer, among other factors—will in turn be attached to the particular behavior being trained, determining the dog's emotional responses to the event. This is not a complicated concept when applied to obedience. It amounts to three simple questions:

- ❧ Is the experience rewarding for the dog? (In other words, is the dog able to meet its goals during the experience?)
- ❧ Is the trainer acting in a happy and encouraging manner during the event? (Is the environment pleasant and reinforcing?)
- ❧ Has a clear, positive association been created in the dog's mind in relation to the behavior being taught?

A positive mood drives positive behavior. A happy and encouraging manner during training yields more effective results. Watch your dog for signs of happiness like solid eye contact and a wagging tail.

These questions must be answered affirmatively in every training session. This is why we only train for five-minute sessions. It is far easier to keep things bright and positive during a short session. The special techniques this book teaches are also designed to produce a bright, positive mood. When obedience is required, we want the dog to be as happy and confident as possible.

Most obedience techniques involve lots of mind-numbing repetitions and the constant use of force. This soon drives the heart out of the dog and produces boredom and resentment. This is not the mood we are looking for, and so we will stay away from such techniques and the long, tiresome sessions that go with them. When positive associations are not present in the dog in relation to the action required, the behavior fails.

Other training systems often refer to distractions, such as other dogs, cats, traffic, crowds, and so on, as the reason that training fails. They claim that the owner has failed to train for and consider all these possible variations in life. It is certainly advantageous to train for special circumstances, but life is unpredictable and we can't anticipate everything that may happen.

The implication of the claim that dogs should be trained to ignore specific distractions, one by one, is that the meaning of the signal to down, for example, alters as the circumstances change. This cannot be so. The meaning of the signal remains the same, and it must be the dog's response that is changing.

Dogs may learn by repetition and association, but they are not motivated by them, or all dogs that have been trained to down by force over and over again would gladly and swiftly down when commanded to do so under all circumstances. Everyday experience shows that this is not the case.

Something else is at play here: mood. The dog whose mood is happy and confident when it hears a signal, whose association to the signal and the handler is one of quiet joy and satisfaction, isn't affected no matter how much "distraction" might be present in a situation or whether the dog has encountered a specific distraction before. We need look no further than the use of the dog in search and rescue or military service, where the circumstances are never the same twice, or anticipatable by dog or handler, to understand that there is more to the dog's mind and behavior than simple repetitions or rigid associations.

When dogs fail to give behaviors that we think we have trained, it is because we have taught the dogs but failed to train them. Moreover, it is because what we have taught them is to hate and avoid their work. We have treated them as if they had no sense of self and have humiliated and degraded them by not accepting them for what they are. We have turned them into reluctant slaves instead of respected partners; we have failed to do unto them as we would want others to do unto us; and we have denied them the opportunity to be happy about their work, be treated with dignity and respect, and have their feelings accounted for.

To sum up, mood is a critical factor in training. Just as human beings must be in the right mood to enjoy dancing and do it well, so the dog must be in the right mood for training to succeed. Furthermore, the dog's mood in training is deeply tied to the trainer's mood. Now let's look at how we can use this understanding of mood to alter a preexisting behavioral problem.

Manipulating Mood in Training

AS AN EXAMPLE of how to manipulate mood in training, let's say that your dog has become dog aggressive and therefore intolerant of other dogs approaching it or you. Many training systems will tell you to restrain the dog or force it into a behavior like the sit, often with a choke chain or pinch collar.

The first thing to point out is that if we restrain the dog through force, we will encounter the fact, well documented by animal behaviorists, that frustration increases drive. Restraint will only make matters worse as the dog becomes more frustrated and therefore more agitated. Second, hurting the dog in any way will be like throwing gasoline on a fire. This is because the dog already fears being hurt, which is usually why it is being aggressive in the first place. Hurting the dog only justifies its fear and concern. Also, we have not solved the problem; we have merely postponed it for a while. Further, we have made the dog's fearful, aggressive mood deepen when what we want to do is to change it.

What we must do here is to put the dog into a behavior through which we can help it alter its mood. The best behavior for this is the down, which is the default "control" behavior (see Chapter 12). If you have created a good, positive down in the dog, you should immediately signal for it on the first sign of aggression toward another dog. If you do not have a good down, you should go home and train until you have a happy, confident, relaxed down. All attempts to handle this situation

Let the Dog Decide | Low-Stress, High-Result Learning

through force alone will not only ultimately fail, but they will also make the situation worse.

Keep the dog in the down until it relaxes into the position and waits for you to release it with the word "free" (for detailed instruction on training the down, see Chapter 9), or to put it another way, until its mood changes. This can take some time, so be patient and know that this technique will serve you well for the life of the dog.

When you see your dog relax and its mood change, immediately signal "free." When you free the dog, get its attention by saying "yes," as explained in Chapter 7, and reward it heavily for focusing on you. When training the down, you reward the dog for going down. Here, assuming that foundation has already been established, you reward the dog for its change of mood.

If it is too hard for your dog to stay down because the other dog keeps coming closer, you must work on this problem in a situation where the other dog cannot continue to approach. This can be accomplished with the help of a friend with another dog or by working in a circumstance where the other dog is behind a fence.

Put your dog in a down every time it shows aggression toward another dog. This initiates a two-stage process over time. First, your dog's own aggression toward the other dog will become a signal for your dog to down. This down in another dog's presence is something your dog will prefer not to do, because it has submissive overtones. Yet the down will lead to a change in mood because you will never let your dog up until its mood has changed.

Gradually the sight of another dog will become the signal for your dog to change to a relaxed mood or for an already relaxed mood to strengthen. A dog in a happy, relaxed mood is unlikely to be aggressive, and your problem is solved. Again, this process will take time and you need to be patient. The change in your dog will be permanent, however, and you will never have to deal with dog aggression again. This is one of many possible examples of how powerful mood is in relation to behavior, and why you need to pay close attention to your dog's mood during training.

The Best Mood for Training

THE BEST POSSIBLE state of mind for any creature is one without conflict, in which it is capable of the most varied response to life's constantly changing circumstances. In another context, the influential trainer Gottfried Dildei has called this state of mind in dogs "the point of greatest mobility." It must be reinforced in the dog more than any other state of mind, if we want to achieve the highest levels of reliability. In this unconflicted state of mind, the dog can as readily give one behavior as another. All things are possible, because stress is almost nonexistent. This is the happy, reliable dog.

The most important thing to remember during training is to create a positive mood. You must focus on this during every session. Remember:

- ❧ If mood is correct, the dog will eagerly learn and give the trained behaviors.
- ❧ If mood is incorrect, the dog will avoid the behaviors and never give them in a way that is reliable.

Once you understand the mood you want the dog to be in to facilitate its learning, you should incorporate that mood into mental visualizations of your dog's successful training.

Visualize Your Dog:
Happy, Confident, and Cooperative

REGULARLY VISUALIZING A goal has proven to be a beneficial technique in many areas, from students' academic achievement to artistic performance and athletic competition. Dog training is also an area in which visualizing your goals, both long and short term, can really help you succeed. You use visualization to keep training on track and to inform you of any unwanted or inadvertent effects produced by your interactions with the dog.

The "journey of a thousand miles begins with a single step," but the wise traveler wants to have a map of the route. We must know where we are going and how to get there. We need to monitor our progress on a daily basis.

The downfall of many training systems is that they fail to describe or account for the dog's appearance during training. Appearance is very important because it reveals the dog's mood to us moment by moment. Does the dog look happy, excited, relaxed, and confident or frightened, depressed, sad, and miserable?

As we saw in the discussion of mood, reliability in the dog is directly tied to its emotional responses during training. It's not hard to understand that a dog that is very unhappy doing a down, for instance, will likely abandon or refuse to give that behavior as quickly as possible. Yet the same dog may need no encouragement to play fetch.

Think of children who love to play baseball or soccer. They do not need to be encouraged to play their favorite game at every opportunity or to submit to the discipline of the game during team play. However, how often are we likely to find these children happily cloistered in their rooms solving math problems? (I want to meet these kids!)

We all want to do things that tend to make us feel good, and so does the dog. Taking the tack that "the dog has to do it regardless" is to turn our backs on a very powerful tool that is at our disposal. It also increases the likelihood that we will produce a dog that is as likely to offer obedience, as the aforementioned children are likely to offer to do math. (But think how different the picture might be if learning math were made highly enjoyable and rewarding to children.)

What we need to do is to create two pictures of the dog in our minds. One we will carry throughout training; it is the picture of our fully trained dog—happy, confident, and cooperative. The second picture will change during training; it is a picture of the dog in a happy, confident state of mind, eagerly giving us the behavior we are about to teach next.

Observe your puppy or dog when it is happily playing to get the idea of what it should look like. Of course the stress of training is bound to show in the dog's appearance at times, but we must work toward the picture we have in our minds and recognize when the dog's appearance

This is what we're looking for: the picture of a happy dog, with ears up, eyes round, and mouth open. A willing worker.

fails to match this picture. The further the appearance of the dog strays from the picture in our mind of the happy, confident dog, the less reliable the behavior we are teaching will be when we are done.

What are the signs that things are going wrong? The recall gets slow and unenthusiastic, the ears flatten to the dog's head, its eyes become slits instead of round and bright, its tail droops, perhaps down between the legs, the shoulders hunch, and the head goes down. The dog may also shiver or shake. Most important, the dog will not look at you or make eye contact. When the dog looks like this, the picture is wrong and you must adjust training.

I know that when a dog's tail is wagging, its eyes are round, its tongue is lolling out, its ears are up, and there is a lightness in its step, the dog is happy. Remember how your puppy ran to you when you first brought it home, how quickly and happily it responded, and make that your reference image as you train. I like to see a dog work quickly because this means it is eager to engage in the behavior.

For example, no one has to encourage a dog to run out fast in pursuit of a thrown ball. But the dog doesn't tend to come back with the ball nearly as fast as it went to get it. This is a common fault in dogs trained to retrieve game. No encouragement was necessary to teach the dog to pursue the duck or bird, and so no time was spent on the dog's state of mind on the retrieve. The result is a slow and inconsistent return, and sometimes, much to its master's chagrin, the dog doesn't return at all.

In competition and in actual hunting situations, this is unfortunately when you see dogs being punished by their frustrated handlers. This punishment is the worst possible, least effective response to the problem. What is really needed is to put the dog in a more positive state of mind when it is returning to its master.

If during training the disappointed and unhappy handlers had visualized their dogs running confidently back to them at full speed, they would have noticed the slow process of depression building up in the dogs. And then they could have altered training to make the dogs happier, and the problem would never have arisen in the first place.

One of the biggest problems in detecting changes in the dog is that they happen slowly. Unless you have the right reference image in your mind, it is easy to lose track of how the dog is doing.

The power of visualization is immense when we picture in our minds what the dog should look like each and every time we train. I picture a quick, happy sit and down, a charging recall that threatens to bowl me over, a high wagging tail, and a big grin on the dog's face. When the picture becomes blurred and the dog no longer looks as it should, I go to benevolent eye contact to build the dog's confidence (see Chapter 7). I change the treats to something special that I know the dog loves. I may switch over to throwing the ball or a rubber chew toy like the Kong brand to the dog who loves to retrieve instead of using food.

Sometimes I suspend training and have a play day or interrupt training for a play time-out and then resume work for a quick two-minute session. I will do everything and anything to keep the dog happy and confident in its work. If I do not do this, all my efforts will be in vain. The dog will hate its job and quickly turn off of doing it.

So make a picture in your mind of your dog happily doing its obedience work. Keep that picture in clear focus, and you and your dog will enjoy all the benefits of visualization.

Delighting the Dog, or the Virtue of Reinforcement on a Random Schedule

THE DOG'S PERFORMANCE during training will inevitably go through peaks and valleys. It helps training progress if we reward peak performances more highly than baseline performances. This makes the peak performances more memorable to the dog and more influential on its future behavior.

In general, the level of reward during training should be random and unpredictable to the dog. This helps keep the dog focused and eager to maximize its rewards with a big win.

For these reasons, when the dog performs exceptionally well, you should pile on the treats, pets, and praise. And then interrupt training for a brief interlude of pure play. I like to act like a puppy myself, getting down to the dog's level for some physical contact, then leaping up and running away a few paces, as puppies do, before getting back down with the dog. I am a serious person for the most part, but in these moments I never shrink from being silly in front of the dog.

Such a dance of joyful abandon will delight the dog and deepen the bond between you. And it has the nice by-product of being good for your own physical, mental, and emotional health, because it will reduce whatever stress you are experiencing as well. So do not feel shy about delighting the dog with extra treats, play, and a little goofy behavior of your own, whenever you feel the urge and its performance pleases you.

Releasing the Dog from Training Work

THIS TRAINING SYSTEM has such a profound psychological effect on the dog that some attention must be paid to the importance of releasing the dog from work with the word "free." The problem that must be addressed is that the dog "locks in" to trained behaviors, especially those behaviors, such as bench work, that represent the escape from compulsion. Once the dog finds safety in the bench, or any other behavior, it may be reluctant to leave it.

This is a bigger problem than one might imagine, because stress builds up in the dog when it stays in the task too long. And then what happens is that sooner or later the dog must release from the task. If it does not do so at our direction and on our terms, it will do so on its own. This is a decision that can obviously create reliability problems. Although my training system is designed to empower the dog's decision making in many other ways, the dog cannot be allowed to decide on its own when to stop and start work.

The solution is to be absolutely clear about the release from work and to engage in training it as seriously as any other behavior. As an example, if you say "free" to the dog when it is on the bench and it does not jump off, you must make it do so (see Chapter 10) and then praise the dog as sincerely as you would for its giving the sit or down.

Sometimes the dog's mood is also strongly affected by this "locking in" to work, and it is necessary to cajole the dog into a different, more playful mood, to free the dog up from its commitment to the behavior. As mentioned, I do this by acting silly and puppylike with the dog, much in the manner of the dance of joy that I recommend in celebration of the dog's best performances. Sometimes a dance of joy to delight the dog is advisable, even when the dog's performance is only middling, to make sure that it does not become preoccupied with its work, like a human workaholic.

TO THIS POINT, we've been considering important general principles for choosing a dog and for good training. Now it's time to turn to the details of actually living with and training your dog.

· PART TWO ·

Day-to-Day Handling and Informal Training

Making the Dog at Home

Training begins the minute you get your dog. As I've explained, in my training system there are only three formal five-minute training sessions a day. The shortness of these sessions accelerates the dog's learning, as we will soon see. But it is important to recognize that the dog is also learning from all its experiences throughout the rest of the day, beginning crucially with its arrival in your home.

When first bringing the pup or dog home, you want to establish the guidelines by which it will live in your home for the rest of its life. The dog's surroundings; its routine for meals, walks, rest, and so on; and its general handling all constitute informal training. If you ignore this fact, informal training can give the dog ideas about how it should behave that can swamp the ideas it learns in each day's three formal, five-minute training sessions.

Fortunately, a little forethought and preparation, and proper early handling, can put the dog on a good footing in your household right from the start.

Dog-Proofing the House and Yard

JUST AS YOU would "baby-proof" your yard and house for the arrival of a new child, so should you "doggy-proof" them as well. Dogs remain emotionally equivalent to a three-year old child for the duration of their lives. Would you let a three-year-old child wander freely about or have access to questionable items?

The house or apartment should have been prepared for the dog before its arrival. All attractive, chewable items like shoes, socks, baseball mitts, toys, newspapers, and so on should have been put away in their proper place. It will naturally help training along enormously if everyone in the family makes a conscious effort to keep things that way.

Outside the House

A secure fence around the yard is a dog owner's best friend, and every dog owner with a yard should have one. The larger the adult dog will be, the more important a fence is. I prefer a real fence to an electronic one, because it protects the dog as well as keeping it inside. But electronic fences can be useful, and the kind of fence you should choose depends on your individual circumstances. A standing kennel approximately six feet by eight feet by six feet high can also be of value, as a way of giving the dog a protected space where it can move around a bit.

Make a point of fencing out any garden areas or plants that you wish to protect. The barrier can be quite a small one. The dog that has been trained with long lines, and so has never been allowed into the garden in the first place, is unlikely ever to be found there digging up your prize roses or tomato plants.

Inside the House

Inside the house you should consider using baby gates to control movement, again just as you would with a child. (If you don't want Grandma's family heirloom Persian rug soaked with urine, don't let the puppy on it!) I like to keep new dogs on nonabsorbent floors like the kitchen floor for the first while, as absorbent surfaces invite elimination. Puppies benefit hugely from this kind of control. It is noninvasive, passive, and covert.

Training Tools Checklist

BEFORE YOU BRING your new dog home, you will want to get a few training tools, which can be found variously at stores that carry pet supplies, hardware stores, and the supermarket. The tools and their use are all described in detail in the sections that follow. Here's a checklist:

- ❀ Flat collar
- ❀ Leash with a clip that attaches to the flat collar
- ❀ ⅛-inch and ¼-inch sail rope for use as long lines inside and outside the house
- ❀ Brass clips to attach the long lines to the dog's flat collar
- ❀ Food treats
- ❀ A clicker
- ❀ A wire or plastic crate to serve as the dog's den at home or while traveling
- ❀ You may also find the Halti head collar useful (see Chapters 6 and 17 for more on this unique, multipurpose tool).

Chews and Other Toys

MANY DIFFERENT KINDS of dog toys are available. You have to use your judgment in buying toys. Those for small dogs may not be appropriate for larger dogs, for example. One important rule to follow, however, is not to use a tennis ball as a chew toy. Dogs love to chew on tennis balls, because compressing the ball is very satisfying. But this easily leads to trouble: The compressed ball can move to the back of the mouth and then expand to block the air channel to the lungs, suffocating the poor dog. Even without that problem, the nylon nap on tennis balls will destroy the enamel on a dog's teeth.

The best chews and chew toys are objects made especially for that purpose, such as the Nylabone brand chews or the Kong brand chew toys. I recommend buying several of these chew toys at once and rotating them every day to prevent boredom in the dog over chew objects. Each day's chew toy can be given to the dog in the morning or left on the floor or in the crate for the dog to discover. The only exception to this is a chew toy that you are going to use to play fetch (see "The Fetch" later in the chapter).

Toilet Training, Meals, and Quiet Time

THE MOST IMPORTANT place to establish in the dog's mind is its toileting area. This is the first place you should take the dog upon arriving home—not into the front room on the carpet but out into the yard where you have defined an area approximately six feet square with small pieces of wood, string, rope, or in some other way that is visible to you and any other family members who will be toileting the dog.

You will always take the dog to eliminate here. This keeps the rest of the yard free of "surprises," when guests are over for a barbecue or the kids are playing with their friends. If you live in an apartment and do not have a yard, you must take the dog to the nearest appropriate space.

In either case, you must stay with the dog until it relieves itself and then praise it highly for its actions. If you say "Hurry up!" in a cheerful voice every time the dog eliminates, hearing these words will eventually become a physiological signal for the dog to eliminate. As I explain later in this chapter, it really does not matter what words you attach to a behavior in the dog's mind. But it is important that you be consistent in the choice of signals and the way you give them.

For at least the first few days, take the puppy out to the toileting area every hour or so and whenever it wakes up from a nap. Later, you should continue to monitor the pup closely when it wakes up from a nap and be aware of how much water it is drinking (pups need a lot of water). You can, however, begin to limit its access to water in the evening to help it last through the night without accident.

Crate Training

THE BEST TOOL for housebreaking the dog, as it is traditionally called, is a wire crate with a nice, smooth floor panel that you use as the dog's den. The crate has many other benefits as well.

Buy a crate of an appropriate size for your dog. I like the Vari Kennel and Furrarri Kennel brands for travel, and an open-wire-style crate—there are many good ones—for in the house. Just like a playpen for a child, the crate is a safe place for the dog to be while you are busy with other things.

The crate helps prevent toileting in the house because the dog does not want to eliminate in its own den. To limit accidents in the house:

- ❧ Keep the dog in its crate at night.
- ❧ In the morning, take the dog out to the elimination area. If it relieves itself, say "Hurry up!" cheerfully, and then praise the dog when it is finished.
- ❧ If the dog does not relieve itself, put it back in the crate for ten to twenty minutes and then try again. This works very well, as the dog sees quickly that it will not be free in the house until it eliminates outside.

I also feed the dog its meals in the crate to build a positive association to containment. I don't want to struggle with a dog that is unfamiliar with or has grown to hate the crate when necessity demands its use at some later date. A dog who loves the crate can safely travel anywhere with you and the family. It is not a cage, but a den, a safe, happy place to be!

Creating these positive associations is part of the dog's training. I seldom close the crate door during the day, and I am always sneaking treats and chew toys into it for the dog to discover when it volunteers to go inside. All dogs love the crate that is kind to them.

After the dog is house-trained, you can make the crate more comfortable with a dog bed, if the weather makes that desirable. But it is best to keep the crate free of absorbent materials, which invite elimination, until the dog understands where it must relieve itself. And remember that the dog's bedding must be cleaned regularly, just like a person's.

Entering and Leaving the Crate and the House

FOR CONVENIENCE AND safety, you cannot let the dog rush out of its crate or shoot through the house door in front of you. Later on, there can be a serious problem if the dog dashes out of a car door, among other possibilities.

Following the same principle as the release from work discussed in the previous chapter, the dog must learn to wait for the signal "Free" before leaving the crate or going through a just-opened door to the outside. Some puppies may be a little shy about leaving the crate, and for them you can use "free" as an encouragement to toddle on out. If the puppy is still reluctant to leave the crate, reach in and take it by the collar and gently pull it out.

If your puppy is bolder, open the crate door slightly, and when the puppy tries to run out, quickly push it closed. When the startled puppy stops in its tracks, you can open the door again and then say "Free" to encourage it to leave the crate. Thereafter, always say "Free" on letting the puppy out of the crate.

At the door to the house, you will ultimately want a formal sit and eye contact. After you have trained the sit (see Chapters 8 and 9), that behavior will become the key that opens the door for the dog, and it will accordingly value the sit at the door highly. Until then, merely restrain the puppy mildly with the leash at the door, get its attention, and say "free" before letting it go in or out the door.

Don't Let the Dog Do Anything Now That You Won't Want the Dog to Do Later

IT IS A wise old view of dogs that you should never give a dog a privilege and then take it away. What they never had they will never miss.

For the puppy, this means that you must not let it do anything now that you don't want it to do later in life—for instance, chew clothes or shoes, which can appear cute when it is small and can usually do less damage; bark, growl, or threaten, unless you intend to seriously train for protection with an expert; jump up on you, which can be dangerous and scary with a 100-pound adult dog; or climb on any furniture, especially the bed. Do not let the dog in rooms that you may not want it in later.

General Control and the Use of the Long Lines

UNTIL TRAINING IS complete, the pup or dog should wear a light line at all times in the house, except when in its crate, and a longer line in the yard or on a walk. This will make handling a breeze and allow you to control the dog completely without its knowledge and therefore without any resistance. Light sail rope of different dimensions works well for the indoor and outdoor lines and will not blister your hands as you use it (see "Training Tools Checklist" earlier in the chapter). You can buy plenty of line at a hardware or home improvement store for a few dollars and cut off lengths as needed. Knot the line to a brass clip. You can also buy these at the hardware store inexpensively, and if you don't lose them, they last a lifetime.

An eight- to twelve-foot line should be attached to the dog's flat collar every time it enters the house. I watch the dog closely at all times and frequently recall it informally to treats, pets, and praise (see "Formal and Informal Signals and Control" later in the chapter). I do not allow the dog onto any carpeted surface, and I use baby gates to help with containment. The dog must learn immediately where it has the right to go in the house and where it cannot. No dog should have the freedom to go where it pleases in the house, anymore than it should be free to run into the street to be hit by a car.

I use my light line to prevent the dog from moving away from me or getting up on any furniture. And I always recall it to praise and reward after stopping this behavior. If you want the dog to get on the couch with you, for example, you can train for this later so the action is under your control. I might add here that dogs define their status by relative body position as well as access to resources. Large dogs with ideas of dominance will become problems if allowed to get on the same furniture as you.

Dogs and Furniture

THE BED IS a particularly favorable position in the house, and I personally never allow any dog to get up on the bed, as this can lead to all manner of misunderstandings. I have had many clients come to me because, while they lived alone, they allowed their dog to sleep on the bed with them. However, when they found a new partner or got married, the dog would not allow the new person on the bed. The dog's getting on the bed and furniture must be totally controlled by you and only allowed through the dog's deference to you, if it is to be allowed at all.

Some years ago I owned a beautiful German Shepherd Dog named Morty, who traveled to dog shows with his professional handler. Unbeknownst to me, the handler allowed Morty on the hotel bed to help build the bond between them while they traveled from show to show. The first time Morty came home from a road trip, he jumped up on the couch with me!

I called the handler to give her a piece of my mind, as he had been trained never to do this. The handler explained why she had allowed Morty up on the bed, and I understood her reasoning. So in fairness to Morty, I made a rule that he could only get on the couch if I put his blanket there first. Morty learned the rule without a problem and all was well, until he began going and getting his blanket and putting it on the couch himself! I ended up having to hide his blanket in a closet to prevent him from doing this trick. Morty was a great dog, and we watched many a ball game together on the couch.

Try to use the long line only with your feet, by stepping on it to restrain or stop the dog. It is okay to grab or pop the line with your hands if the dog's back is turned, but drop it immediately and step on it before the dog looks at you. Remember that a pop on the line should be just firm enough to interrupt the dog's behavior and no firmer.

When you first free your dog on the long line, it can be helpful to offer the dog extra encouragement, such as a ball, to come when called.

Except for these covert uses of the line, try to pay no attention to it at all in your interactions with the dog. After a few days of wearing the line, the dog will begin to ignore it, too. You might consider playing fetch (see "The Fetch" later in the chapter) or some other game when you first attach the line to the flat collar to help condition the dog to it.

If the dog chews the line a little bit now and then, pay no attention and simply replace the line when needed. If the dog obsessively chews the line and it quickly becomes damaged, however, admonish it to stop with a sharp pull on the line, and recall the dog to lots of positive attention from you. It would be preferable never to let the dog see you use the line to interrupt its behavior, but if you must, you must.

The objective of the long line, remember, is to control the dog's movement and behavior covertly while reserving your hands for praise and comfort. This keeps the dog from becoming "hand shy," which heightens the dog's resistance to coming when called. The worst mistake that people make in training a dog is to use their hands for control. With the long line attached to the flat collar, the dog will never know where the line ends, the dog will not see you holding the line with your hands, and you will never have to chase the dog if it misbehaves.

For example, inside the house, suppose the dog charges the door when someone knocks or rings. In that case:

❧ Step on the line as the dog begins to charge, and turn your back as it hits the end of the line.
❧ Keep your back turned briefly, so that the dog can see that you apparently have nothing to do with its experience. Then turn around so that the dog can see your empty hands, and bend down and call the dog to you with open arms.
❧ When the dog comes to you, reward it with praise, pets, and a treat. Try to make brief eye contact with the dog during this process of praising, petting, and treating (for more on eye contact, see Chapter 7).

If the dog jumps up on visitors, pull on the line from behind with enough firmness to pull the dog down off the person. Likewise, if the dog chases the cat, a young toddler, or young child, step on the line and let the dog stop itself at the end of the line with the force of its own running. Then recall the dog to you. When the dog comes to you, give a treat, praise, and pets.

You can use a long line in the house to covertly control behavior such as stealing food. Using a long line to control movement and behavior lets you reserve your hands for praise and comfort, which keeps the dog from becoming "hand shy."

Once your dog has made its move, pull on the line just firmly enough to knock it off balance.

Drop the line before the dog turns around and call it to you for treats, pets, and praise. Your dog will learn that trying to sneak food is unsuccessful and that coming to you is highly rewarding.

If the dog chews on the furniture, a shoe, or other inappropriate object, step on the line if the dog runs away as you approach or "pop" the line with your hands from behind the dog and then step on it to restrict its movement. Remember to try never to let the dog see you holding the line. Then bend or kneel down, and recall the dog to you with open arms to receive a treat and/or praise and pets.

Employ the same techniques outside the house, where the dog's natural tendency to roam around will offer many opportunities to teach it that the safest and most rewarding behavior is always to pay attention and stay close to you. The dog that is never allowed to roam in the first place and does not believe it is possible to roam will not be found down at the neighbor's house digging in the garbage. And you won't be hearing from an angry neighbor or the local animal control officer!

The process of roaming begins with the dog's first innocent wanderings away from you in the backyard. This often happens while you are distracted or engaged in some other behavior, for example, when you are gardening or talking to a neighbor. It is at these times that the long line is your greatest ally.

A long line will help prevent chewing on slippers or any other inappropriate object.

Using the light line, catch your dog from behind and pop the line just hard enough to get your dog to drop the slipper.

Call your dog back to you for praise, pets, and reward. The lesson is learned.

Stand on the line and pretend nothing is happening. Ignore the dog's struggles, and never allow the dog to move away with intent to do anything that does not involve your influence, like chase a cat or a squirrel, dig a hole, or play with another dog without permission. The dog will never know why it cannot do these things, but eventually it will abandon the idea that they are possible.

This is not only for your convenience but for the dog's safety and your peace of mind. As training progresses, you will be able to give your dog plenty of opportunities to romp with you and other dogs and to explore its surroundings. But just as you would never want your young child to chase an attractive ball into the street, you don't want your puppy to chase an attractive squirrel into the street either, or to think that it can go wherever it pleases whenever it pleases. The statistics on dog injury and death confirm that this is wise. Don't put yourself through the heartbreak of losing a dog when it is run over by a car because you left the dog too free to roam at a young age.

Whenever the dog runs away from you and bumps the end of the line, recall it to you every time and reward its coming with praise, pets, and treats. Never call the dog, however, if you are not yet standing on the long line. This guarantees that the dog cannot refuse to come when called. Lure the dog to you with a treat, if necessary.

In a few days, the dog will begin to believe that it is not safe to run from you and that paying close attention to you and staying near you are highly rewarding. You will notice the dog start looking back to you every time it thinks about moving away from you. Praise this response every time.

In general, you want the dog on a long line at all times during training. But there are, of course, situations and circumstances where this is not appropriate, as when you are walking the dog on a busy street. You can always take the long line off as necessary and just walk the dog on its leash.

Making Yourself the Focus of the Dog's Positive Associations

AN IMPORTANT GENERAL training principle underlies the use of the long lines: Every unpleasant experience or failure the dog experiences should be followed by a positive experience connected with you. You must develop the habit of encouraging the dog to come to you after every incident and rewarding it for doing so. Some of these incidents will be ones that you covertly arrange as part of training, like stepping on the long line if it chases a squirrel. Others may occur naturally, such as when a young dog pokes its nose into a bees' nest or is slapped on the nose by a cat.

This will create two positive results. One is that the dog will be inclined to come to you whenever things go wrong, as opposed to avoiding you. Second, because each incident is followed by friendly and rewarding behavior from you, it will make it even harder for the dog to detect your covert control of its actions with the long lines. The dog should be learning that it is only safe when near you, and that other places are not safe.

In short, there are two opportunities to shower the dog with affection that should never be missed. One is after the dog suffers an unpleasant experience. The other is when the dog performs correctly by complying with your wishes.

The Right Treats for the Right Occasion

IN THE THREE formal, five-minute training sessions, you will use special treats as described in Chapter 7. In informal interactions around the house and yard like those we've just been describing, it is best to reward the dog with little biscuits or dog cookies. During training I find it useful to put a bowl of little dog biscuits in every room where the dog will be, so that I can immediately reward the dog for its good behavior. And I put a bigger bowl by the door, because of the many issues connected with entering and leaving the house and the arrival of visitors (see Chapter 17).

The closer the reward is to the behavior, the stronger the positive association with the behavior that forms in the dog's mind.

Formal and Informal Signals and Control

IN HANDLING A dog, there is a distinction between casual, informal signals and control-oriented, formal signals. During formal training you will teach the dog to respond immediately and without question to specific word signals. To clarify the difference for the dog between formal and informal signals, separating those instructions that must be obeyed to the letter from more casual directions, I use some German or German-like words in my training system. These formal signals are used when the dog has my full attention and I am prepared to follow through in the situation.

For example, if there is traffic nearby and the dog must stay closely by my side in the heel, I use the formal signal "fuss" (rhymes with "goose"), as opposed to the more informal signal "close." If there is some hazard to the dog's movement and I need it to go into a down, I use the word "platz," (rhymes with "cats") rather than the informal phrase "lie down."

Formal training signals can be any words that are not in common use and that the dog will not frequently hear in other contexts. This helps ensure that the dog does not become confused about the meaning of the signals. You can make up your own private signals, if you like, or you can use the list that follows. The signals I use for formal training (my apologies to anyone who knows the German language; I spell the German words phonetically and use an English language pronunciation for them) are as follows:

- *Here*. Come to the "front" position.
- *Sitz.*– Sit.
- *Shtay.*– Stand. (Although "Shtay" rhymes with "stay," the origin of the term in my training vocabulary is the German word "steh," meaning "stand." In this training system, you do not need a "stay" signal; instead you train the dog to remain in the sit, stand, or down, until you release it with the word "free" or signal for another behavior.)
- *Platz.* (Rhymes with "cats.") Down, the control behavior.
- *Climb.* Signal to climb on bench for obedience practice or to get into a car or other vehicle.
- *Place.* Go into kennel or crate, or get on dog bed.
- *Yes.* Look at me (make eye contact).
- *Close.* Walk by my side or stay nearby.
- *Fuss.* (Rhymes with "goose.") Do a proper heel, or come to heel from the "front" after recall.
- *Wrong.* Mild admonition to change behavior from something unwanted.
- *Ah–ah*. Stronger admonition to change behavior from something unwanted.
- *Free.* Release from any signaled behavior, such as "Platz," and release to get out of a vehicle or the crate, or pass through a door (an important safety measure).
- *Aus.* (Rhymes with "house.") Drop it! Let go with the mouth!

It is counterproductive to use formal signals if all I want is the dog to settle down while I watch the ball game or engage in other everyday activities. In these situations, like any other owner, I simply tell the dog, "Go lie down." If the dog gets up after half an hour and wanders into the kitchen to visit my wife, for instance, there is no concern about its breaking a rule of training, which would then result in a loss of overall reliability.

This would also be true of a situation where I wanted the dog to stay near me in the park. I don't want to use the formal recall signal "here" in this situation, which is trained to produce a high-drive charge into a sit directly in front of me, but rather a casual suggestion on the order of "Hey, boy; c'mon, buddy," with the expectation that the dog return to my vicinity and hang around.

One of the most often used signals the dog hears is its name. If you are going to use the dog's name in any situation involving casual control, you must attach a strong positive association to its name. This means rewarding the dog when you use its name and it responds properly by paying attention to you. It also means that you must never admonish the dog by name or punish it if you have used its name in relation to the unwanted behavior. Failure to reward the young dog when you use its name leads to the older dog's ignoring its name being called, a frequent occurrence that can be observed in any dog park.

Hand Signals

DOGS BY THEIR nature are keen observers. Your dog would much rather gather its cues from watching your actions than listening to what you say. Unfortunately, the dog can make any interpretation of your actions that it pleases, which is why it is so hard to keep a dog in a stay while you move about, for example. The dog will also notice any movements you make when training it and prefer to respond to these body motions rather than focusing on and listening to your verbal cues.

This means that you must train the dog to focus on your verbal cues first and foremost. You must offer the dog as little visual information as possible during the teaching phase in particular. Hand signals must never be taught to or used to control the dog until the dog responds perfectly to verbal cues.

The Fetch

ONE OF THE things I like to teach early in training is the fetch. I don't see this as formal training but as a fun game to play during the day. The fetch has immense value in training, however. Dogs will naturally chase any attractive object or small creature, and even large ones. But bringing a captured prize back to us involves an act of willing service. This is an attitude we want in the dog.

Here is how to teach the fetch to a young puppy:

- ❧ Crumple up a sheet of paper to use as a ball. I sit down with a pad of paper so that I can crumple up a fresh sheet into a ball whenever I need one.
- ❧ Put the puppy on the light line and get down on the floor with it. I like to sit about three feet away from a wall in the kitchen. Sometimes I will put my legs out and press my feet against the wall, creating a triangular space between my legs where I position the puppy.
- ❧ Tuck the line under you, leaving just enough slack for the puppy to chase the paper ball. You don't need much slack, perhaps three feet or so, because you want to keep the dog in the triangular space formed by your legs.
- ❧ Wiggle the paper ball in front of the pup to excite its interest, and then throw the paper ball against the wall so that it bounces back toward your lap. Crumpled-up paper makes a good ball for beginning to teach the fetch indoors for three reasons: It won't damage anything, it is light and easy to retrieve, and it will not snag in a puppy's needlelike teeth. Throwing the paper ball against the wall and having it bounce around animates it and makes it a more attractive object to chase.
- ❧ When the pup catches the ball, entice it back to you by cooing and by clapping your legs with your hands.
- ❧ If the pup does not return, use the light line to make it do so by tugging sneakily on the line from under your leg. Tug with little pops that are just forceful enough to encourage the pup to come to you.
- ❧ When the pup returns, praise it heartily and pet it.
- ❧ Hook a finger under the pup's flat collar, and with your other hand, begin to wiggle the ball in its mouth to encourage it to release it. Say "aus" or "out" while you do this to teach the dog the signal for releasing an object from its mouth.
- ❧ If the pup pulls and refuses to release its "prey," do not tug on the paper ball. Let the hand wiggling the ball move with the pup's mouth, and instead hold the pup in place with the finger on the other hand that is hooked under the collar. Never

exert pressure on the pup's mouth. The pup will eventually make a chewing motion with its mouth, and you can pop the ball out. If the paper gets soggy, simply crumple a fresh sheet into a new ball.

❧ As soon as the pup releases the ball, say "free" and throw the ball against the wall again immediately as a reward for the release. The intimacy of this game, with the puppy chasing and bringing the ball into your lap, where it can snuggle and be petted, and immediately getting a fresh chase as soon it releases the ball will build immediate, eager compliance later on, whenever you need the dog to let go of something in its mouth.

It is perfectly normal for a dog to refuse to release objects from its mouth that it has captured. It is also normal for growling to accompany the refusal. This is a fundamental behavior in the dog that has to do with survival in the wild. The most compelling argument for the dog to release an object is that the release will immediately produce the chase game and another chance to capture the object. This satisfies the dog's instinctive prey drive.

Playing the game of "give it to me and I will give it back or give you something better" with a young pup will prevent possessiveness problems in the future. If the dog is very possessive, I reward releasing the ball with the best possible treats. When training a dog that is tough or dominant or both, I trade treats for objects for an extended period, sometimes until the dog is a year old.

Never pull on something that is in a dog's mouth unless you intend to protection-train the dog with an expert trainer. Exert any pressure necessary to keep the dog from jerking away from you (again, this should always be the minimal pressure required) with one or two fingers hooked under its flat collar, and do not grab or hold the dog directly. Let the dog pull against the flat collar as hard as it wants while you wiggle the object loose from its mouth.

Do not play tug with your dog, especially if you have children. This will encourage the dog to bite and so should only be done in protection training with the participation of an expert trainer.

One of the most counterproductive things that people do with dogs is to tease them during the fetch game by pretending to throw the ball or other fetch object and then holding it behind their backs. Repeated teasing in this way makes a dog prone to aggressive mouthing, nipping, and even biting to protect its prized possessions and to refusing to return the object during fetch. The dog will do unto you as you have done unto it.

If you offer a ball or object to the dog, you must throw it. Hiding or withholding it is cruel to the dog and creates problems that the dog may pay for with its life, if it bites someone seriously.

As your pup becomes larger and better at the fetch game with the paper ball, you can switch over to a Hacky Sack, the small beanbaglike toy that kids kick in the air with their feet. You will probably not want to throw the Hacky Sack against the wall. You can toss it across the room, or at this point, you can move the game outdoors, gradually increasing the distance that you throw. You can stay with the Hacky Sack while the puppy is small and then transition to a rubber chew toy like the Kong or a sturdy rubber ball, like a lacrosse ball, that the dog cannot compress in its mouth. Never use a tennis ball (see "Chews and Other Toys" earlier in the chapter) or anything similar that the dog may choke on.

Always stop the game of fetch while the dog is still excited about playing. This will maintain its enthusiasm for the game the next time you play. Pick up the fetch object and put it away. Do not leave it down for the dog. This is a game that you want the dog to be dependent on you to play, and the fetch object (in the dog's mind, the prey object) must belong to you and you alone. The dog must earn the pleasure of capturing it again by returning it enthusiastically to you.

A Day in the Life

DOGS ARE VERY adaptable creatures and will ultimately conform to any lifestyle. But here is an outline of how to give your dog a good start in your home.

I start the day with the dog in its crate from the night before. I like to putter around a bit to make it clear to the dog that noisemaking or other forms of complaint will not get it out of the crate. I then open the crate door and make the dog wait until I say "free" to let it out, as described previously.

I immediately put the dog on the leash and take it outside to the elimination area and encourage it to do its business with a "hurry up." Saying these words consistently will soon produce the desired results.

If the dog does not eliminate, I put it back in its crate for twenty minutes and then take it outside to try again, remembering to say "hurry up." After the dog eliminates, I praise the dog and bring it back inside. And then I immediately attach the long line so that I can free the dog for some quiet social time with me, followed by a quick training session, while still retaining covert control of its movement.

After the training session is done, I remove the long line and put the dog back into its crate for breakfast and at least half an hour of quiet time. After that I take the dog back out to its toilet area for another opportunity to eliminate. Some dogs prefer to eat first before emptying their bowels.

If the dog does not eliminate, I put it back in its crate for twenty minutes and then try again. After the dog eliminates, it is time for the dog to hang out for a while on the light line, which I use to control all its movements as described previously. You should take a young puppy out every half hour or so to eliminate, particularly if it is drinking a lot of water.

An hour to an hour and a half is usually about as much as a pup can take before it needs a nap. So it's back in the crate for a time-out for the puppy, and a break for me. It is also a good idea to put a new older dog in the crate for a time-out. Whatever the dog's age, this teaches the lesson that "freedom" is not to be taken for granted but is rather a privilege that you and you alone control.

When the dog awakens, or I wake it, we go outside to the elimination area. If the dog fails to eliminate, it goes back into the crate for another twenty minutes as described previously.

After the dog eliminates is often a good time for a training walk. I let it explore and see the world but never allow it to pull on the leash. I use the dog's name to call it back to me constantly during this walk, rewarding the dog with a treat each time, because short recalls on the leash build great recalls off the leash.

When we return home, I do a training session and then put the dog back into the crate to eat or for a time-out. Young pups will often have another short nap.

In about an hour, I take the dog back out of the crate to its elimination area and follow the same procedure as previously outlined. Then the dog goes back onto the light line for some social time with me in the house or onto the long line if I'm out in the yard.

Whenever the dog is out of the crate, I keep an eye on it and interrupt any unwanted behaviors with the long line. And I interact with the dog using informal language, rather than the formal language of the three 5-minute training sessions. You must never lose sight of the fact that the dog is learning, and in effect being trained informally, whenever it is out of its crate. If you are not careful, this informal training will undermine the formal training of specific behaviors that you do in the five-minute sessions.

For example, while keeping the pup or the yet untrained dog around the house, I would only call the dog by name, not use the formal "here." I would say "lie down" rather than the formal "platz." And there would be no reason to use such formal signal words as "fuss," "shtay," "climb," or "sitz" at this point in training. Once I have begun to develop good eye contact (see Chapter 7), I might say "yes" occasionally, but only if I am prepared to reinforce the response with a treat.

If I need to concentrate on some work at my desk or in the kitchen, I can put the dog on a tie-out nearby with a chew toy and/or a dog bed. The tie-out can be as simple as looping a leash around a table leg before attaching it to the dog's flat collar. Or the long line could be used in a pinch. But during training it is better to take off the leash and the long line, which invite chewing when the dog is kept in one place (this is also why you remove the long line when the dog is in its crate), and use a light chain for a tie-out.

For a permanent tie-out, clip a light chain about as long as the distance from the floor to the dog's withers (the high point of the back at the base of the neck between the shoulders) to an eyebolt secured to a wall stud or a heavy piece of furniture. Clip the other end of the chain to the dog's flat collar. The permanent tie-out is only "permanent" while the dog is being trained. You can remove the eyebolt when training is complete.

If the kids are coming home at a particular time after school, I put the dog up for a rest in preparation for the serious play that will soon occur. I get the dog out in the proper manner, and if the kids are old enough, I have them do a click and treat session with the dog (see Chapter 8). Then I stand back and let the fun begin! If there are no kids about, it's time for some more social time with me and any other adults in the household.

Children and Dogs

INTERACTION BETWEEN CHILDREN and a dog must be monitored carefully. If you have any doubts about the dog's gentleness, it should not even be allowed. This is why it is so important to choose an appropriate dog to bring home in the first place. For help with a puppy that mouths and nips, see Chapter 17. This problem must be solved before the dog is allowed to interact freely with the members of the household.

The next training session will happen before the dog has its final meal of the day (three meals for puppies and two for older dogs). Before that, I like the dog to hang out in the kitchen on a tie-out or the long line while I prepare the family's dinner, so that it learns that its food never comes from that source. Just before dinner I do a training session and then put the dog in its crate to eat at the same time the family does.

After dinner is usually a social time for the family and the dog, including a walk or play after a visit to the elimination area. As evening comes on, I put the dog on a tie-out nearby on a blanket or dog bed, while the members of the family watch television, play a board game, read, and so on. Again, the younger dog is taken out at half-hour intervals to eliminate and returned to its crate if it fails to do so.

I often do another training session during this family time. The kids love it, and so does the dog. I know this makes four in one day, but fun is fun. And who can resist!

Now we must take the dog out for its evening toilet, remove its water bowl from the crate (unless it is hot inside) and bed the dog down in the crate for the night.

This system modifies as the dog becomes more responsible and responsive to training, but the crate time, although diminished, is never eliminated from the routine. Every dog needs to know how to be calm and happy in its crate at all times.

If no one will be at home with the dog during the day and you have space in a yard to do so, build a kennel and put chew bones and play toys in with the dog when you leave. If not, crate the dog and try to have someone come home during lunch break to get the dog out for a while. Dogs do very well in crates during the day, as they settle down in their own little dens for sleep and quiet time. Do more with the dog in the morning, and make the evening the biggest time of the day with both the walk and training sessions happening during this time.

A perfect day!

BY FOLLOWING THE advice in this chapter, you can quickly get your dog settled into your home. But the dog's environment also includes contact with the world outside your home. The next chapter explains how to handle the dog's walks and its socialization to people and other dogs.

Introducing the Dog
to the World

Walking the dog and taking it to the park or on other outings can be great fun. But these activities can also be ruined by battles of will with the dog, or by its discomfort with other people or with other dogs. Fortunately, the same general handling techniques that you follow at home will also help prevent, reduce, and eliminate problems with the dog elsewhere.

Walking the Dog

MORE DOGS SPEND their lives chained up or locked in a yard because they cannot walk properly on the leash than for any other reason. When I lived in town, I often watched out my front window as people from the neighborhood walked their new puppies to the local park. The scenario always went something like this.

For the first few weeks the owners walked down the street smiling and happy with their bright young dogs. The pups looked curiously in all directions, alternating between sniffing all the new smells and running back to their owners for reinforcement and pets.

During the next few weeks, the first signs of discomfort began to show on both the owners and pups. The pups pulled a little harder on the leash in an attempt to move toward something of interest, and the owners strained at the effort of controlling the now more confident pups. The pups also displayed less and less interest in returning to their owners for security and affection.

From there things went steadily downhill. The larger a pup grew, the harder it pulled on the leash, and the more contorted the owner's face and body became in the effort to control the dog. The joy of walking with the new puppy had become a daily struggle, with the dog literally dragging the frequently shouting, gesticulating owner down the street.

After an owner and dog reached this point, I saw them pass by less and less often. Finally, it happened that I sometimes saw the owner walking to the park, but now without the dog. Because I am always interested in meeting new dogs, I made a point of introducing myself to people and their dogs when they first passed by my house or I first saw them in the park. When I saw these folks walking alone and asked about their dogs, the reply was always more or less the same:

"The dog pulls so hard I just can't walk it anymore. I tried going to training and using a choke chain or pinch collar, and that seemed to work for a while. But the dog just pulled harder in the end anyway. I hated to do it, but I just gave up."

"Where is the dog now?"

"Oh, in the backyard."

And so it went.

The real problem in these situations is that people have allowed their dog to pull toward the things it wants, rather than teaching it to accept a loose leash as the only successful way to get there. Restraining the dog with a tight leash runs afoul of a biological fact I discussed earlier: frustration increases drive. The harder the dog pulls, the more frustrated it becomes. This produces more energy or drive in the dog, and it pulls harder and harder as its frustration increases.

Following the method in this book with a new puppy will do a lot to teach the dog to walk on a loose leash. Using the long lines, establishing benevolent eye contact, and doing short, upbeat training sessions with lots of pets, praise, and treats will condition your dog to pay close attention to you. The long lines in particular will prepare the dog for the reality that pulling never succeeds. For many dogs and their owners, continuing in this fashion—sustaining and enhancing the dog's attention on the owner—is all that will be needed to produce happy, relaxed walks on the leash.

Begin by taking walks solely for the purpose of leash training, using a leash attached to the flat collar. This is a good opportunity to "double–rig" the dog with the long line and take advantage of any attempt to misbehave by the dog when the leash comes off. The dog may get charged up with nervous energy while you walk it on the leash, for example, and then bolt as soon as you remove the leash. This gives you another opportunity to exercise covert control and show the dog that the nicest, safest, most rewarding place to be is right by your side. The walks can be on any schedule that is convenient. Never use a choke chain or pinch collar. Carry plenty of treats and

- ❧ Call the dog to you for reward and eye contact whenever it looks at you. (As Chapter 13 explains, these short recalls from the end of the leash will build great recalls off the leash.)
- ❧ If the dog tries to pull away from you even slightly, pop the leash just firmly enough to put the dog slightly off balance. (Again, do this only with the leash attached to the flat collar, never with a choke chain or pinch collar.)
- ❧ Do not say anything to the dog when you do this.
- ❧ If the dog looks back to you when you pop the leash, call it to you, stoop down and make eye contact, and then reward the dog with treats, praise, and pets.
- ❧ Walk here and there, making frequent turns. At first you should never take more than a few steps in any direction, and you should always change direction if the dog looks away from you for any period of time. The dog must not be able to anticipate where you are going, or even be conscious that you are going anywhere in particular. Just wander about. This is truly a case where it's not the destination but the journey that matters.
- ❧ Do not jerk the dog's neck when turning, as alpha-dominance-based, classical conditioning training systems instruct you to do with a choke chain or pinch collar. Just casually change direction.

If the dog falls behind you when you turn, encourage it to your side by slapping your hip with your hand and reward it as it comes up beside you.

If the dog forges ahead of you, change directions, and then reward it as it comes up beside you.

Maintain a happy, encouraging demeanor throughout the walk. As you teach the dog more about the "yes" signal to look at you (see Chapter 7), you can apply this on your walks together.

Your dog will soon know that a walk never involves pulling on the leash. The dog will decide that pulling on the leash is a losing behavior and will abandon it.

The product of working eye contact and developing the dog's focused attention on you: a loose leash, and an effortless heel. The dog wants to be at your side.

The Halti Head Collar

ALTERNATIVELY, YOU CAN take the dog on its first walks using the Halti brand head collar, and then transition to using the leash attached to the flat collar. The Halti is a great tool for teaching a dog how to behave well on the leash, and its gentleness is part and parcel of its effectiveness.

For a detailed explanation of how to use the Halti and why it is different from other head collars, see Chapter 17.

Socialization and the Dog Park

EVERY DOG NEEDS socialization to humans and dogs both for its own well being and that of others. To become well socialized, the dog must have contact with a variety of people and dogs from an early age.

Contact with people enables the dog to interpret human behavior correctly. This tends to neutralize the natural protective and territorial instincts that can cause difficulty when the dog feels it must defend its owner or family in nonthreatening situations. It also reduces the naturally occurring fear that some dogs may have of strangers from outside their "pack."

Likewise, exposure to other puppies and dogs at an early age enables the dog to interpret the behavior of its own kind. This will prevent the appearance of fear and aggression in your puppy. Careful attention by you on the dog's early visits to the dog park will teach it to avoid fighting and keep it from becoming overly concerned with its place in the world of dogs.

Socializing the Dog to People

TO TRAIN THE dog's proper socialization to people, you need a fairly busy place like a public park, a shopping mall, or even the front of a big apartment building. If you live in an urban neighborhood, a brief walk around the block can bring the dog into contact with a number of people. People and children have an affinity for puppies, and few of those you encounter when you take your puppy out in public will decline the opportunity to pet and greet it.

Do not overwhelm the dog with too much noise and other stimuli too soon, however. You should carefully work your way up to walking the dog in very crowded, noisy, and bustling circumstances.

I like strip malls for socialization because of the way they are arranged. The bigger stores that draw most of the traffic are in the center, with smaller, less frequented stores at either end. This allows you to take the dog through a progression of exposure to more and more people.

On the first visits, I keep the dog at the end of the strip mall where there are the fewest people. As the dog becomes comfortable with the experience of meeting and interacting with people, we move toward the center of the mall and the front of the biggest, busiest store.

Likewise, I gradually increase the length of time I keep the dog at the mall. The first visit may only be five minutes, particularly if the puppy seems overwhelmed by the experience. Over the course of a few to several visits, we work up to staying twenty minutes or longer.

Here's how to get the dog used to meeting people:

❧ Take lots of treats and welcome all those who wish to interact with the puppy.

❧ As people approach the puppy, crouch down beside it to restrain it from jumping up on them. You want to show the dog that sitting for strangers produces treats. You can ease the dog into the sit while hooking one finger through its collar and scratching its chest. This prevents the pup from pulling on the leash and creating drive problems.

❧ If your puppy is frightened by people approaching, ask the people to stand two or three feet away. Then give the people a treat and let the dog approach them, which will reassure and embolden it.

❧ If someone comes by with another dog that frightens the puppy, pick the puppy up and turn away until the other dog has passed.

❧ Do not be worried if the puppy becomes momentarily concerned by a stranger's body language, another dog, or a rattling baby carriage or shopping cart. When this happens, you may see the puppy's eyes narrow, its ears flatten, and its tail go down below its rear, and it may hide behind you. It is natural for the puppy to have moments of uncertainty and anxiety in this experience. You have brought the puppy into a new environment with strange people precisely so that it can learn to handle this mild stress and recover from it.

- ❧ Remain neutral, and wait for the puppy to regain its confidence and its natural curiosity to take over.
- ❧ If the puppy remains frightened and anxious for more than a few moments, however, do not prolong the experience. Reassure the puppy with benevolent eye contact and a treat, and then take it home to work on more benevolent eye contact. You can always try again another day, when the puppy is feeling more secure.

After half a dozen to a dozen or more of these sessions, the puppy should happily greet strangers and be unbothered by the hustle and bustle. You can then take the dog to all sorts of new places, among all sorts of people, without worry.

Socializing the Dog to Other Dogs

THE DOG PARK is a natural place to take the pup to meet its own kind. This is very important, as most dog aggression occurs when an inexperienced dog is unable to interpret the behavior of other dogs correctly. Dogs' aggressive body language and vocalizing are meant to prevent fights and make them unnecessary, so it is important for the dog to interpret these signals correctly.

Going to the park does not mean the dogs can be left to work things out on their own. You have to watch the behavior of all the dogs, including your own, and intervene if aggressive posturing goes beyond the display stage and becomes physical or overly threatening.

Trips to the dog park are thus filled with potential problems as well as learning opportunities. To ensure happy, relaxing times in the dog park for you as well as the dog, you need to pay careful attention to how the dog experiences its early visits there. If you socialize your dog properly, however, it will become more and more able to fend for itself socially and coexist peacefully with other dogs.

The most common mistake people make in using the dog park is to control the dog tightly with the leash while getting there and then give the dog total freedom once they arrive. If you do this, you end up looking bad to your dog, compared to the fun that can be had romping with other dogs, who never restrain it or tell it "No!"

You will look especially bad to the dog if this strictly disciplined walk to the dog park is the first contact it has had with you after being cooped up in the house, the yard, or its crate for an extended period. Under these circumstances it's no wonder dogs are reluctant to return to their owners when playtime is over. You have shown the dog that you are no fun at all compared to its own kind.

There are several ways to prevent this problem from occurring or resolve it if it does:

- ❧ Play with the dog for a while before going to the dog park or dog run.
- ❧ Carry a large bag of treats and gratify the dog for paying attention to you as you slowly make your way closer to the dog park. Have the dog on the leash and the long line. For reasons of practicality, you may want to use a ten-foot line for this purpose rather than a longer one. And in more urbanized environments, you may not want to have the dog on a long line as you walk along the street. In these cases, attach the long line when you reach the park or an open area where you can use it effectively. You can also use a retractable leash, like the Flexi brand, but keep in mind that this will not allow you to control the dog covertly.
- ❧ When you first enter the area, keep your dog on the leash and recall it to you, with eye contact, from the short distance of the length of the leash. These short recalls on the leash build great recalls off the leash.
- ❧ Let your dog greet the other dogs while on the leash, and keep recalling it to food treats and praise.
- ❧ Take the dog on several such visits before unleashing it in the dog park for the first time. When you do release your dog, keep it on the long line. Make a show of unleashing the dog and saying "free."
- ❧ Stand on the long line. If your dog tries to dash away from you heedlessly, it is in for a surprise. When the dog hits the end of the line, recall it to you by name or the formal signal "here," depending on which stage of recall training you have reached (see Chapter 13). Remember to reward and praise the dog for coming to you. You are going to let the dog run around with the other dogs in due course, but you want to instill the habit in your dog of looking to you first to check for permission.

❧ After you have freed your dog in the dog park, recall it frequently to eye contact and reward. At first give the dog thirty seconds to a minute or so between recalls, never letting it become so deeply involved with the other dogs that it forgets about you or will not recall.

❧ Once the dog is used to this routine, start to ask for a simple response, like the sit, for example, and reward the dog's successful performance with lots of treats and praise. You want your dog to see that you have much more to offer than any dog could ever provide. As you build on this initial pattern of behavior in the dog park, the dog will develop a habit of looking to you frequently, which you should encourage with praise and with more treats and pets when the dog comes to you, whether or not you have called it to you.

❧ If the dog ever fails to respond to your call or to check in with you regularly, remove it immediately from the area and get its focus back on you with benevolent eye contact (see Chapter 7). There will be many opportunities to take the dog to the park and let it play with the other dogs.

❧ Do not spend too long a period of time in the dog park, especially when your dog is young, in order to keep it from becoming overly concerned with its status in the world of dogs. After twenty to thirty minutes, leash the dog and return home or move on to a walk or other activity with the dog. If you are involved in a conversation with other dog owners that you cannot break off at this point, leash the dog and keep it by your side, with periodic benevolent eye contact and treats, until you are ready to leave.

❧ After you leave the dog park or when you arrive back home, spend a few minutes playing with the dog yourself or working on benevolent eye contact, again to ensure that you remain the center of its universe. And then put the dog in its crate or kennel for a rest. By the way, quiet times in the crate or kennel are a great way to bookend both training and walks. This gives the dog an uneventful contrast to the stimulation and reward that it enjoys during training sessions and walks with you.

Dog Friendships and Rivalries

ONE OF THE most important considerations in owning a dog is that it not become overly concerned with its relationship with other dogs. In this regard it is vital to understand how dogs express dominance and submission to each other and the serious nature of what can look like harmless, if rough and tumble, play.

See Chapter 15 for a discussion of how dogs should play. In brief, you do not want the dogs to wrestle and play fight. This behavior is actually a deadly serious struggle over status, and you must step in to end it as described in Chapter 15. You must also step in if you see your dog getting locked into eye contact with another dog, with neither dog looking away to defuse the tension. This is a sign that a fight is brewing.

Instead of being in opposition to each other, no matter how playful it may seem, the dogs should quickly progress to acting together in mutual play, moving as one to investigate a sound or smell, and during breaks in the action standing side by side or ignoring each other rather than standing face-to-face. Bowing the legs to solicit play, tail wagging, looking away from each other, and standing side by side are all positive signs that indicate the dogs have no agenda other than to get along and enjoy themselves. If the dogs paw the air or paw mildly at each other but do not progress to closer physical contact and wrestling, that is also okay.

Not all dogs are friendly and of a peaceable disposition, and this can be said of their owners as well. Even if your dog is not physically injured, it can be frightened and intimidated in a lasting way by encounters with aggressive dogs. Your dog could then itself become aggressive out of fear and anger or become sadly withdrawn and hesitant around its own kind.

Upon nearing or entering the dog park, take stock of the situation before even considering taking your dog inside or letting it off leash. Look around and identify the dominant and/or aggressive dogs in the dog park. In effect, you are about to expose your dog to an already formed pack. If you do not yet know how dominant or submissive your own dog's temperament is, the dog park will make that clear.

This is yet another reason why trying to be the alpha pack leader to your dog is an ineffective approach. The alpha dogs in the dog park will play that role much more convincingly than any human being ever can.

On your first visit to a dog park, you will likely find that the other dogs have already solved their status problems and formed up as a pack. Your dog will be the odd one out and will need special watching. As you observe the pack, look especially for any dog with its hackles (as mentioned, the hair on the back of the neck and shoulders) raised. This indicates a fearful dog that is prone to unpredictable aggression. If you see such a dog in the dog park, it may be wise to postpone your own visit to the dog park until after this dog has left it. For more on fear-driven aggression in dogs, see Chapter 16, "Difficult Dogs."

Recognizing Dominance

YOU CAN RECOGNIZE the dominant dogs in any pack by their body language when establishing status. A dominant dog will often carry its tail high, well over the back, walk "on tiptoe," and approach other dogs directly face-to-face. It will attempt to put its head and neck over the necks and backs of other dogs, put its paws on their backs, or even mount them. The dominant dog may also show its teeth and emit a low growl.

On meeting a more dominant dog, the less dominant dog will often lick the first dog's face to express its friendliness and acknowledge its inferior status. The less dominant dog may also bow its legs and drop its head or even fall on the ground and expose its belly. The dominant dog may simply accept this as its due, without any obvious response, or it may lick the less dominant dog in return or sniff it a little. In either case, after such a meeting, all will likely be well between the dogs.

If you want and expect real work out of your dog, never allow another dog to dominate it. In any case, never let other dogs dominate your pup or dog unduly. Not all dogs can be king or queen, and your dog may be well down the status list, but that is no reason for it to be constantly harassed during playtime. You can assess the situation best by watching your own dog's body language. If it is in distress, it will show this with flattened ears, narrowed eyes, a hunched back, and lowered tail.

"Chasing" can be a beneficial method of diffusing aggression, especially if it is reciprocal. Make sure your dog has plenty of room to escape during a game of chase and that these games gradually wind down rather than being endlessly repeated. The dog's long line should not interfere with its play; in forty years of training, I have never seen a dog become tangled in one except when the end of the line was tied to an immovable object rather than being left free. However, use common sense and remember that it is always a good idea to keep your eye on the dog's activities in the dog park so that any problems can be nipped in the bud.

The problems of the dog park are not solely the result of the dogs' interactions by any means. The other half of the equation is how their owners behave. Some owners may simply not be aware of their dogs' behavior and what it means. You want to socialize with those owners who carefully monitor their dogs and are quick to step in if they see something inappropriate, as professional dog walkers do.

If another dog begins to act in an inappropriate way toward your dog, watch to see if the owner steps in and stops it. If the other dog owner ignores the situation, address the other dog by saying "Shoo, go away, go home," or "No!" If there is no response from either dog or owner, put your dog on the leash immediately and leave the area. Again, there will be plenty of days to go to the park and work on socialization. It doesn't have to be done all at once.

One last bit of advice on your interactions with other dog owners: Don't waste time arguing with them about anything having to do with dogs. Many dog owners, especially ones with problematical dogs, are deluded about their knowledge of dogs and dog training. As in any situation, there are always some know-it-alls around who will never listen to reason. Some of them are more aggressive and overbearing than their dogs.

Let any advice they offer go in one ear and out the other, and take no offense. Just walk away quietly and enjoy your dog. As you and your dog frequent the park, you will soon find other owners and their dogs with whom you feel compatible. One of the great things about taking your dog to the dog park is that both you and the dog get to make new friends.

IN THE NEXT chapters, I'll explain how to begin the dog's formal training.

· PART THREE ·

Formal Training

7

Building Benevolent
Eye Contact

Before exploring how to build benevolent eye contact with your
dog, the first step in its formal training, let's briefly consider how
all of formal training should proceed. For the best results, you should
start training when the puppy is between seven and eleven weeks old.
This is the time of maximum imprinting on the dog's consciousness and
personality. After the eleventh week, whatever problematical tenden-
cies the dog may have will be harder to moderate. But any dog under
one year old should respond quickly and well to my training system.
For guidance on training the older dog or a dog of any age—even a
young puppy—that comes from a shelter, see Chapter 3.

You will need the following training tools:

- 🐾 A flat collar and leash
- 🐾 A light line about ⅛-inch thick and eight to ten feet long to
  attach to the dog's collar inside the house
- 🐾 A stouter line about ¼-inch thick and thirty to sixty feet long
  to attach to the dog's collar outside the house
- 🐾 A clicker
- 🐾 Plenty of treats

Treats can be cut-up pieces of cheese or hot dogs or any nutritious
human food that the dog loves (I'll explain in the next paragraph and

upcoming sections why you should use human food). Don't be puritanical on the dog's behalf. Using lots of treats is only a stage in training, and you will not have to depend on them for long. But in the meantime, the more mouthwatering and plentiful the treats are, the better. A plastic sandwich bag will hold enough treats—twenty to thirty—for each training session, as well as for use on the dog's first walks on the leash.

As I mentioned in Chapter five, little dog biscuits are good as rewards during informal training and handling over the course of the day. But the treats for formal training must be much more delectable, such as those suggested above. They will in turn make the formal training sessions intensely memorable. These treats must not be anything chewable, which distracts the dog, but true melt-in-the-mouth and swallow-at-once items. You cannot train effectively with kibble, biscuits, or chewable packaged dog treats.

The Training Schedule

YOU SHOULD TRAIN your dog in three five-minute training sessions a day: morning, afternoon, and evening. Schedule the sessions before the dog's meals. If it is slightly hungry during training, the treats it gets for good behaviors will be more meaningful.

As I discussed in Chapter 2, short training sessions are for the benefit of your focus and concentration as well as the dog's. At first, you may even find it best to train only for two to three minutes at a time. If at any time in the training session the dog's body language indicates that it is losing concentration or becoming fearful, anxious, or confused—ears and tail down, whimpering, and so on—bring the session to a close with praise, pets, and treats. Likewise, if you are distracted or upset, or if you are becoming frustrated with the dog, you should also bring the session to a close with praise, pets, and treats.

Throughout each five-minute session, you want to see the dog happy, alert, and eager to win more treats. And you want to show the same positive mood and eagerness to let the dog discover how to access reward.

The young dog has a short attention span. Continuing to train after the dog has lost interest or can no longer focus makes training uninteresting. This builds an indifferent attitude in the dog toward the work, as you in effect reinforce the dog for not paying attention. You can also lose enthusiasm yourself quite quickly in the beginning of training, especially if you haven't yet learned to read your dog's subtle responses in its body language and "nothing seems to be happening."

Three five-minute training sessions divided between morning, afternoon, and evening also mean that the dog experiences long periods of downtime between sessions where it cannot earn special, multiple rewards. This makes the dog eager to win treats when it can. During the five minutes of each training session, the dog only has a limited number of chances to succeed and the quick, fun training with lots of mouth watering treats stands out in its mind. The dog also sees clearly that it needs you to make this winning happen.

It is essential that you show the dog a friendly picture of yourself while training. This means keeping all threatening behaviors to a minimum:

- Do not stare at the dog unless you are building benevolent eye contact with plenty of treats, as discussed in the next section.
- Try to keep your body language soft by avoiding standing squarely in front of the dog, facing it down so to speak, with a very erect posture, like a drill sergeant facing down a new recruit. Instead, keep your shoulders round with the shoulder nearer the dog slightly lower than your other shoulder.
- Do not train if you are in a bad mood, nervous, or tense. This will be transmitted to the dog and create a negative association to the task you are teaching.
- Having the proper nonthreatening body language is far more important than any specific technique. Getting down on the ground and making yourself small delights the dog and makes you less threatening.
- Finally, begin training indoors where you can ensure that there are no distractions. Move outside to the yard or a nearby field or park as you and the dog gain confidence in each other and in the training.
- Always remember that there is no schedule for results, that every dog learns at its own pace, and that the smartest dogs can sometimes take the longest time to train.

Establishing and Building
Benevolent Eye Contact

BENEVOLENT EYE CONTACT is at the heart of my training system. Its value to both you and the dog is immeasurable. Your first training sessions should therefore concentrate on building good eye contact.

As we saw in Chapter 2, it is not in the nature of dogs to stay in very close physical proximity to dominant forces such as human beings, so you must teach the dog that it is safest when it is closest to you. Begin by using food treats to draw the dog into the "area of influence" around you.

I like to get down low with puppies, sometimes even sitting or lying down on the ground, and by using food as a lure, I encourage the dog to commit its body to mine by touching me with its chest, not just its legs. As the dog becomes more comfortable with this exercise, you can begin to hold the food in a way that causes the dog to look more and more directly at your face and eyes.

In the beginning this can be from an arm's length and for a short duration of time, even if it is only a second or two. Gradually you bring the dog's face quite close to your own while it makes direct eye contact with you for an extended period of time—in the end, as long as five minutes.

You achieve this by drawing the dog closer as it becomes more comfortable with the stress of eye contact over the course of several training sessions. An excellent technique is to sit down in a chair, draw the dog between your legs with a food treat, and feed it more treats from there. When you do this, instead of cutting the food into small bits, cut cheese or hot dogs into long strips and let the dog nibble at the end of the treat while maintaining eye contact.

Hold the food in a way that causes your dog to look you in the eye. Do not touch your dog. Eye contact must be a volunteered behavior.

Build eye contact and reinforce the "front" with plenty of practice and treats.

Remember that every dog learns at its own pace and there is no set number of sessions in which it should learn to do anything. As the dog becomes able to tolerate greater closeness with eye contact, vary your body language by sitting up taller, standing with knees bent, and eventually standing straight up so that you are looking down at the dog as it sits before you.

Make yourself smaller to lessen the threat to your dog while you draw him closer to you and maintain eye contact.

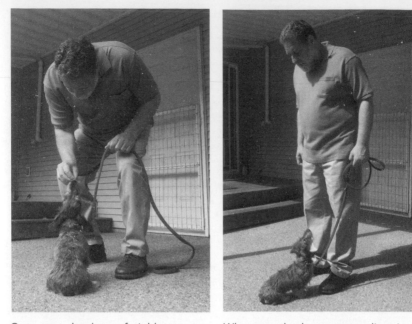

Once your dog is comfortable, you can move to the next step where you are more upright and your body language is more threatening.

When your dog has overcome its natural concerns, you can stand upright and stare down at it. Your dog will be seeking eye contact, and you can drop food to it from your mouth.

This is called the "front" position. This is the most threatening position for the dog in relation to its owner. If the dog can be comfortable here, it will be comfortable anywhere. It is also the position we recall the dog to and represents the last link in the behavioral chain that is the recall.

When you begin working on eye contact, you do not want to space out separate treats but rather to feed the dog more or less continuously while it is making eye contact with you. Once the dog is comfortable with staying close to you while you are standing erect over it, begin dropping small bits of food directly onto its face from between your lips, and then from your mouth, rather than feeding with your hands.

The reason for dropping the food from between your lips and then from your mouth and thus the reason for using nutritious human food that you won't mind eating if you swallow a bit of it by mistake is as follows. So long as your hand is in the picture, the dog will tend to focus on your hand and its movements, rather than on your face and eyes. This will keep you from establishing the full, trusting eye contact that you want with the dog.

Older dogs can be very threatened by eye contact. Approach your dog in the least threatening way by turning sideways, looking away, and then offering the food.

Make yourself small and allow your dog to stay at a distance, only looking occasionally at its face.

As your dog becomes bolder, you can stand more upright, still allowing the dog some distance.

Bolder still and with growing confidence, you can draw your dog tight into your body, the position resembling the "front" more and more with every repetition.

Full of confidence, your dog can now come close into the front. To continue building trust, begin to drop food to your dog from your mouth.

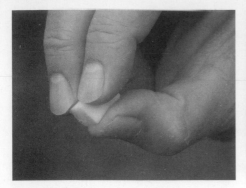

The proper method for holding food: notice how the fingernails protect against the dog's teeth from both above and below. Squeeze your fingers together, oozing the reward out into the dog's mouth. You want the dog to suck and lick at the food and gain gratification slowly but steadily. Your aim here is not to "feed" so much as to create an association.

A hot dog cut into a long, thin strip makes an excellent treat for working eye contact while sitting down with your dog's head in your lap or with the beginning dog where you are stooping or kneeling down to draw the dog close to you.

Equally important is that in hiding the food in your mouth you are changing it from what animal behaviorists call a primary inducement to a secondary inducement. This crucial step helps you move away from depending on treats to win the dog's good behavior and enables you to achieve the reliable obedience that is necessary for the dog's safety and your peace of mind.

If you find a food that motivates the dog, like all-beef hot dogs, unpleasantly greasy, you can cut them up and microwave them on a paper towel. Or you can use cheese or some other food that the dog enjoys and you can at least tolerate. If you still cannot tolerate putting the food in your mouth, you can hold it under your chin, without using your hands. This can be quite messy, and your results will be limited by your inability to hide the food completely.

Finally, if you feel that this too is not acceptable, you can hold the food in front of your face before dropping it to the dog. But keep in mind that this will make it more difficult to reap the full benefit of benevolent eye contact and will also make it harder to train the dog to respond to obedience signals when you do not have a treat. In what follows, therefore, I am going to assume that you have found a human food treat that is highly desirable to the dog and that you don't mind putting in your mouth.

Catching the food that you drop from your mouth becomes a fun game, and the dog quickly learns to catch it in the air. If the dog is being inattentive and not catching the food most of the time, attach a leash

An excellent way to build benevolent eye contact is to hide treats in your mouth. With your dog close in front, make sure that the food is visible and holding the dog's attention. You can keep your dog there for longer and longer periods of time, then drop the food. As your dog becomes more confident of being rewarded, you can begin to hide the food in your mouth, alternately bringing it out to be seen and removing it from sight before dropping it.

to the flat collar and use it only to prevent the dog from picking food off the ground that it has failed to catch. The dog will soon learn that to win the treat it must pay close attention to your face and eyes.

At first you should hold the food to your lips, where the dog can see it. But over time, shift to hiding the food in your mouth. Again, by moving the treat from a place where it is plainly visible to a place where it is invisible, you turn it from a primary inducement to a secondary inducement. This plays a large part in the dog's movement from working for a reward to working for its own reasons. You should practice this exercise until the dog will consistently make eye contact when there is no visible reward. So long as the dog can see the treat, benevolent eye contact will be incomplete.

Gradually keep the dog in this position—the front—for longer and longer periods of time, delaying gratification by withholding the reward, but always feeding before the dog breaks off eye contact. I like to stand with the dog in the front and continuously drop treats from my mouth.

The longer the dog is able to hold your gaze, the more treats you should give as a reward. You must walk a line between convincing the dog that waiting longer and longer pays off and losing the dog's attention because reward does not appear to be forthcoming. Likewise, you as the trainer must remember that the dog must win reward at every trial, because it will only repeat successful behaviors.

The general point to keep in mind is that consistency is crucial in training your dog. If the dog's behavior does not trigger a rewarding response from you, the dog will abandon the behavior you are teaching or, even worse, tune you out.

Always make eye contact and feed the dog when you call it to you, inside or outside of the five-minute training sessions. As mentioned, at first the eye contact on recall can be very brief and it should never be forced on the dog. As the dog grows comfortable with more extended eye contact during training sessions, you can extend the eye contact during recalls throughout the rest of the day. If you do not have food available at any time when you have recalled the dog, you must make a big fuss over it and heap on the praise and attention.

Saying Yes to Benevolent Eye Contact

A FINAL ELEMENT IN building benevolent eye contact is to attach the word "yes" to it as a signal. You do this simply by saying "yes" whenever the dog looks at you. Soon the word itself will signal to the dog that it should look at you. This is a valuable tool for later training because it allows you to focus and freshen the dog's attention in the course of a training exercise.

WHEN YOU COMPLETE this initial stage of training, you will have the most responsive dog you have ever seen. You will have created a dog that always comes to you when you call and stays in close proximity to you at all times. This effect will be for the life of the dog and is a very powerful tool.

Using the Clicker

In **Chapter 2** we discussed how a clicker can become the dog's conditioned reinforcer. You use the clicker to do operant conditioning. This is a stress-free way to teach the dog a pleasurable association with a behavior that you desire.

Clicker training is a valuable stage for the vast majority of dogs. But as I explained in Chapter 2, you should skip or shorten this stage and start training on the bench as described in the next chapter if your dog:

- ❖ Does not respond eagerly to food treats during the first few clicker sessions.
- ❖ Is very dominant aggressive or sharp shy. (See Chapter 16 for guidelines on recognizing and dealing with dogs that fit these descriptions.)
- ❖ Is systems wise. (Again, a systems-wise dog is one that anticipates or avoids negative outcomes in training and resists and resents being manipulated in this way.)

Dogs that have been trained with classical conditioning involving high levels of compulsion are commonly systems wise. Overly forceful and frequent compulsion soon loses its shock value. The dog expects compulsion and tries to avoid it by avoiding the obedience situations in which it is being hurt.

Dogs that are very strongly active or passive resisters (see Chapter 16 for descriptions of these extreme personality types) also commonly become systems wise. These dogs may ignore the clicker or walk away, respond to it only as long as it suits them, or even show aggression out of resentment. If you begin clicker training, and your dog displays any of these behaviors, it is best to put away the clicker and go on to bench training.

Again, however, the vast majority of dogs will benefit enormously from clicker training. Here's how to do it.

Teaching without Commands

WITH THE EXCEPTION of the word "free," as I'll explain in a moment, the initial stage of clicker work is nonverbal. You do not tell, command, instruct, or coach the dog to do anything verbally, and you do not even name the desired behavior.

The reason why you refrain from naming behaviors, or giving "commands," as they are incorrectly called, is that at the start of learning a behavior, all dogs are nervous and concerned. The dog is eager to please you to win the reward of your praise, a pet, and a treat. But at this time, it is neither adept at the behavior nor confident in it.

You therefore do not want to create an association in the dog between its initial feelings about the behavior and its poorest performances, which always come during the learning phase, and the name of that behavior. If you wait until the dog has perfected the behavior before naming it, you will then create an association in the dog's mind between its best possible work and that word signal. This strong association between the dog's best performance and the name of the behavior will last for the dog's lifetime.

Begin this training in a safe, quiet place where there are no distractions. The first step in using the clicker is to condition the dog to associate the clicking sound with the provision of a treat. You do this simply by clicking and then immediately dropping a piece of food onto the floor or ground. You click and drop food until the dog shows that it recognizes that the click sound means a treat is forthcoming.

This process can take from a few minutes to a day or two. Once it is complete, you begin to use the conditioned sound of the clicker as a reinforcer to tell the dog when it has given the correct behavior. For example, you can begin to use the clicker to reinforce good recalls. When the dog arrives after you have called it, click the clicker and give a treat.

For new behaviors, like sitting, standing, or lying down, you can either wait until the dog offers the behavior on its own or use a food treat to lure the dog into the desired position in the same time-honored way that you can get a puppy to sit for a cookie. It is much better in the long run, however, if you can be patient enough to let the dog run through its repertoire of possibilities and offer the desired behavior on its own. When we human beings discover something for ourselves, we find it much more memorable, interesting, and exciting than if we passively receive that information from an instructor. Likewise, if we become conscious of being manipulated into doing something, we resent it a little, even if we are ultimately rewarded for that behavior.

It is the same with all creatures, and it is especially true of dogs. The long lines are so useful, because the "no's" the dog experiences don't seem to come from you but are part and parcel of how the dog discovers the world to be. So with the clicker, try to refrain from instructing or coaching the dog verbally. If you instead let the dog discover for itself what behavior wins a reward, it will make the dog's learning much more powerful and effective.

If your dog keeps persisting in one behavior, like sitting, when you want it to learn to lie down for a reward, there is no harm in luring the dog into position with a treat. But thereafter, try to let the dog run through its own options, so that the dog has a feeling of self-control, self-actualization, and free choice in accessing reward. We want our dogs to be masterful in good behavior, with as little overt control from us as possible.

Here's how to do it:

- ❧ As soon as the dog sits, stands, or lies down, click the clicker and toss a treat on the ground.
- ❧ Toss the treat away from the dog so that the dog will have to move to get it. As you throw the food, say the word "free."
- ❧ Now wait until the dog offers the complete behavior again. It won't take long.
- ❧ As soon as the dog gives the desired behavior, click and throw a treat as before, saying "free" as you throw.

The reason you can say "free" right from the start of training is that this signal means exactly that: The dog is free to do what it wants, and there is no worry that the word will be contaminated by anxiety or confusion in the dog's mind.

Continue this process with the dog until you can reliably predict that it will volunteer to sit, for example. This is a one-for-one ratio: The dog gives one sit, and you respond with one click and treat.

This will probably only take one training session. But if it takes more sessions, that's okay. Every dog is different, and every dog has to work out problems at its own pace. In subsequent training sessions, you want to raise the ratio of behaviors to click-and-treats as high as possible. So you begin to withhold the click and treat to get a two-for-one ratio.

A two-for-one ratio means that the dog will sit twice, for example, and you will click and treat only once. Here's how to begin increasing the ratio of behaviors to rewards:

❀ First let the dog give a complete behavior, such as sitting, and click and treat as normal, one for one, remembering to say "free" when you throw the food.
❀ Then let the dog give another sit.
❀ While it is still sitting, walk around behind the dog. The dog will get up and follow your movements. It will be inclined to do this because it is expecting a treat and watching you intently to see when you will drop it.
❀ When the dog begins to follow you, stop, turn toward it, and wait for it to sit again.

As soon as it sits the second time, click, say "free," and drop a treat on the ground.

Now you have two sits for one click-and-treat. Patiently continue this process until the dog will give four sits for one click-and-treat, or a ratio of four for one.

After this is accomplished, you should put the dog on a random schedule of reinforcement. This means that you constantly vary the number of behaviors the dog gives before you click and treat. You should also vary the reward for the dog by dropping as many as five pieces of food for a behavior. This keeps the dog's interest sharp and focused.

One Lesson at a Time

IN EACH FIVE-MINUTE training session, you should only try to work on one behavior (the sit, stand, or down), until the dog is completely confident in it. Although your first training goal is benevolent eye contact, you can work on sits, stands, or downs at the same time. Spend thirty seconds to a minute on benevolent eye contact at the beginning and end of each session. This leaves three to four minutes in between for clicker work, which is plenty of time to get the twenty to thirty clicks and behaviors that you should try to achieve in each session.

Divide the behaviors up among the three daily training sessions. For example, you can do sits, with reinforcement of good eye contact, in the morning session; stands, again with reinforcement of good eye contact, in the afternoon; and downs, not forgetting to reinforce good eye contact, in the evenings.

When training is more advanced, you can run through many behaviors in sequence without the dog becoming anxious, fearful, or confused.

9

Naming Behaviors and Strengthening Benevolent Eye Contact

Once the dog will give approximately four sits, stands, or downs for one click followed by a treat, it is time to attach a signal word, often mistakenly referred to as a "command," to the behavior. You achieve this through further use of the clicker:

In Chapter 5 I explained the value of using special signal words, like "sitz" for "sit," "steh" for "stand" and "platz" for "down," that the dog will not frequently hear in other contexts. For the sake of clarity, however, I am going to use the normal words—sit, stand, and down—in describing how to train the named behaviors in this and subsequent chapters. In training your dog, you should use whatever formal signal words you have chosen.

Naming Behaviors

LET'S BEGIN WITH sits. At the start of the training session:

- ❧ Click and treat only for the sit so that the dog knows what behavior is going to win a reward in that session.
- ❧ Don't instruct the dog in any way; let the dog run through its options. Sit may well be the dog's first choice, but if not, be patient and give the dog time to figure out what the winning behavior is.

- Next, let the dog offer the sit, and then pass in front of the dog and walk away from it to get it to follow you. It will be inclined to do this because it is expecting a treat and watching you intently to see when you will drop it.
- When the dog begins to follow you, stop, turn toward it, and wait for it to sit again.
- As the dog's rear drops toward the ground, say the word "sit."
- When the dog's rear touches the ground, click the clicker, then simultaneously throw a treat on the ground and say "free."

After the dog has eaten the treat, repeat the same process for the rest of that five-minute training session to reinforce the association between the signal word "sit" and the behavior. Don't forget to wrap up each training session with some extra treats, pets, and benevolent eye contact. Then put the dog in its crate for half an hour to reflect on what it has just learned and dream of winning more rewards in the next training session.

Follow the same procedure, in separate training sessions, for naming stands and downs. You can work on sits in the morning, stands in the afternoon, and downs in the evening. In any case, it is essential that you give the appropriate signal word, whatever it may be, as the dog performs the behavior, not before it begins to do so.

From this point on, only click and treat for a sit, stand, or down that has the signal word attached to it. This will establish a strong link in the dog's mind between three things: a specific signal word, a specific behavior, and a reward.

It will also deepen your dog's focus on you. Your dog must pay closer attention because it is now dependent on you to give the verbal cue, the signal word, if it is to succeed and win reward with its behavior.

To achieve this in the sit, for example:

- Let the dog sit, but do not say the word "sit," and do not click and treat.
- The next two times the dog sits, however, say the word "sit" as it sits, not before it begins to do so.
- Click as the dog completes the sit; and then throw a treat on the ground and say "free."
- Use the click to mark the behavior, and say the word "free" to signal the end of the behavior.

You now behave in two different ways in front of the dog:

A. You let the dog sit without saying anything and without clicking the clicker and then giving a treat. You will have to move about, preferably behind the dog, to cause it to break out of the sit.
B. You stop moving and let the dog begin to sit. As the dog begins to sit, you say the word "sit"; as it completes the sit, you click the clicker; and then you throw a treat on the ground and say the word "free."

Keep alternating between one A and two Bs for the rest of the five-minute training session. Then end the session, as always, with some extra treats, pets, and benevolent eye contact, and put the dog in its crate for a little while to reflect and dream of future victories.

As training progresses, vary the pattern in which you withhold or supply the signal word and the click followed by a treat. Over the course of a five-minute training session, the dog should give a behavior without hearing the signal word and receiving a treat 30 percent of the time. The other 70 percent of the time it should give a behavior and simultaneously hear you say the signal word, hear a click as it completes the behavior, and then see you throw a treat and hear you say the word "free."

The dog will soon recognize that if it offers a behavior without hearing the signal, the click followed by a treat never comes. The dog will recognize that its successful behavior depends on hearing the signal and will then begin to wait for the signal to come. This is a perfect illustration of the value of training to the dog's understanding. The dog not only learns that a certain behavior can earn a treat but the special conditions under which that is possible.

It does not matter how many sessions it takes your dog to learn this. Allow your dog the freedom to learn at its own pace.

Once the dog has achieved this new understanding, you begin to give the signal word *before* the dog does anything. If you are devoting a session to the sit, you now say the word "sit," wait for the dog to sit, click as it completes the sit, and then throw a treat and say the word "free."

You are back to a one-for-one ratio of reinforcement. That is, every time you say "sit" and the dog sits, you click and treat. As in phase one training, you now begin to raise the ratio of behaviors to every click followed by a treat, as follows:

- Say the word "sit."
- When the dog sits, say "good dog" and "free." You will probably still need to move about before the dog breaks out of its commitment to the sit.
- Say "sit" again.
- As the dog completes the sit and its rear end touches the ground, click the clicker; then throw a treat and simultaneously say the word "free."

You now have a two-for-one ratio, or two signaled "sits" for one click followed by a treat. Continue this training—again, it doesn't matter how many sessions it takes—until the dog is on a four-for-one ratio: four signaled sits for every click followed by a treat. Then put the dog on a random schedule of reinforcement as described in "Teaching without Commands" in Chapter 8.

When training behaviors, you should try to reward the dog's best performances. In advanced training for certain dog competitions, accuracy is more important than speed. But for the training in this book, you want to reward the quickest, most unhesitating behaviors, because that is what will make the dog's responses most reliable.

Repeat this in separate sessions for stands and downs. You can train signaled sits in the morning, for example, signaled stands in the afternoon, and signaled downs in the evening.

You should now keep the dog on a random schedule of reinforcement for all behaviors until eye contact is strong enough to take the dog to the bench. You can continue to use the clicker to teach other new behaviors, if you wish. My daughter Rosalee likes to teach the dogs to "high-five," and after we watched the *Garfield* movie, she taught her dog to dance as "Odie" did in the film. This was all done with the clicker. There is no end to the fun you and your dog can have. Just use your imagination!

Strengthening Benevolent Eye Contact

BENEVOLENT EYE CONTACT must become stronger in order to prepare the dog for the stress of climbing the bench. This means keeping the dog in eye contact with you for longer periods of time over the course of several sessions, during which you supply plenty of praise and continuous reward.

Building benevolent eye contact with your dog

To counter and prevent handshyness, begin to pet the top of your dog's head while feeding and maintaining eye contact.

As the dog grows more comfortable, swing your hand past your dog's head while maintaining eye contact and feeding. This exercise reduces the perceived threat by your dog.

While maintaining eye contact:

❧ Begin to pet the dog on the top of the head with gentle strokes from the forehead back over the ears. You will probably see the dog's eyes narrow as you do so, and the dog's ears may also go back or down.

❧ Respond by praising the dog in a soft, kind voice and feeding it continually. Remember to say the signal word "yes" frequently.

- Carry on with this until the dog's eyes remain more open and the ears stay up or pop back up after your hand passes over them. These are signs of relaxation and comfort in the dog.
- Once the dog is comfortable with being stroked on the top of its head during eye contact, begin to swing one hand over its head while you praise and feed it. This will remove all hand shyness from the dog and help it to cope with other people, especially children.

During walks, you will often meet people who want to interact with your dog. Unfortunately, human and dog instincts can be at odds here. An adult instinctively reaches out to pet the dog on the top of the head or a child runs up waving his or her arms in excitement, the dog recoils or shows aggression (both behaviors are fearful responses), and what should have been an easy, pleasant encounter for everybody becomes a difficult one. This exercise will help your dog cope with these stressful experiences and remain calm.

In the course of strengthening benevolent eye contact, you should gradually show the dog more forceful body postures by standing more squarely in front of it and approaching it more directly. When you recall the dog, for example, you should transition from squatting down to standing up tall and square onto the dog, with your hands at your sides, while you look straight down at it sitting in front of you. Keep the dog in this front position for longer and longer periods of time while making eye contact. During eye contact, reward the dog with food dropped from your mouth.

The goal in this work is to make the dog comfortable with maintaining eye contact for at least one to two minutes at a time while in the front. You also want to continue conditioning the dog to look at you every time you say the word "yes."

If at any time you see signs of worry on the dog while you show more forceful body posture, such as flattened ears, narrowed eyes, lowered tail, and/or a slow, reluctant recall, you should get down at the dog's level to make eye contact and feed the dog simultaneously to relieve the stress. Patience with this process will pay off enormously when you begin training the dog on the bench.

Climbing the Bench

Chapter 2 explained how the bench provides a painless way of taking away the dog's mobility to train it to produce behaviors reliably on signal, which is necessary for your peace of mind and the dog's safety. The bench is also where the dog will first experience compulsion and learn how to escape it by being compliant. Before you begin to use the bench, it may help to review "Compassionate Compulsion: Using the Bench" in Chapter 2.

This phase of training involves a strong tactile approach, and for the first time, you will guide the dog into position physically. You will also begin training all three obedience behaviors—sit, stand, and down—in the same training session.

During operant conditioning with the clicker, the dog saw all behaviors as voluntary and engaged in them purely to satisfy its own desire for a reward. This is a powerful and useful technique, but it will not produce reliability in the dog.

With the bench, you introduce the dog to the idea that not only can it continue to win reward, but it can also escape the indignity of being put in place by you. The dog gets to choose, and you shape the training to let the dog decide between responding to the signaled behavior or losing its dignity and independence of action when you move it into position with your hands.

In this crucial phase of training, the dog learns to escape from compulsion into compliance. In fact, the dog learns to escape from even the

Bench training will help build reliable responses in your dog. Benches should be appropriate to your dog's size: little dog, little bench; big dog, big bench!

possibility of compulsion and secure its own safety, comfort, and high levels of reward in freely chosen compliance with your wishes. If you do not do this training, you can never be confident that the dog will not choose to chase a squirrel into the middle of the street or engage in some other instinctive behavior that puts it at risk. Without learning how to escape compulsion in compliance, the dog will never be reliable.

Bench Work and the Traffic Safe Dog

BENCH TRAINING HAS many positive results. One of the most important is that it helps control getting the dog in and out of vehicles, whether cars, taxis, pickup trucks, or boats, and helps the dog be comfortable in new situations that may make it nervous or frightened. Every year a large number of dogs are injured or killed because they jump out of cars without permission as soon as the door is opened. You will now have absolute control of this very dangerous situation.

I spoke about compassionate compulsion in dog training in Chapter 2. Here I want to emphasize that the dog experiences even the gentlest touch as compulsion. The slightest pressure on the dog's rump to get it to sit, for example, inevitably triggers resentment and resistance. As you may already know from experience, that gentle touch soon becomes insufficient and before long you have to push down with increasing force to get the dog to sit. This is a losing proposition if ever there was one.

When you move into bench training, you must recognize that if you touch or move the dog in any way, except to pet and comfort, the dog will experience this touching as compulsion. Every time you use compulsion, you risk the dog going into a defense response—submission, avoidance, or aggression—and this is something you never want the dog to do in relation to you.

Keeping in mind that it is impossible to train reliability without the use of compulsion, we want to use the least compulsion necessary and maximize its positive effect on the dog. My method accomplishes this by teaching the dog that it has control over all compulsion that it may encounter, as well as control over access to any and all rewards and affection that come from you. By teaching the dog to escape compulsion in compliance, you put the basic decision-making process under the control of the dog.

Here's how to do it:

- ❧ Attach a leash to the dog's flat collar. In this situation, you do not need the long line on the dog. You can leave it on the ground beside the bench and clip it back onto the flat collar when you finish a session's bench work.
- ❧ With the dog at your left side, walk the dog to the front of the bench.
- ❧ Say the word "climb," and immediately pull the dog up onto the bench with the leash. Pull gently but steadily, and gradually increase the pressure, using the minimal amount of force necessary to get the dog on the bench.
- ❧ As soon as the dog is on the bench, stop pulling on the leash, releasing all pressure on it, and say the word "yes" to make benevolent eye contact. This prevents the dog from falling into any defense behavior.
- ❧ Dogs will often drop their heads at this point (an attempt at avoidance or submission) and resist eye contact. If this happens,

hold a food treat directly under the dog's nose and lure its head up until it makes eye contact.

❧ Once you have eye contact, feed and praise the dog. Calm and secure the dog on the bench by using lots of reward. Then release the dog to jump down off the back of the bench by saying the word "free."

Step 1: Getting ready for the climb. Make sure you have a grip on your dog's leash.

Step 2: Give the signal to climb and begin to gently pull your dog onto the bench.

Sept 3: Immediatly make eye contact and feed your dog.

Step 4: When your dog is comfortably in the sit, continue to feed and make eye contact.

❧ If the dog doesn't instantly come down off the bench, gently but firmly pull it off with the leash, using the minimal force necessary to get the dog off the bench.

❧ Throughout bench training, use only the minimal amount of force necessary and do not tug or yank on the leash. Put only slow, even pressure on the leash. This pulling on the leash represents overt control rather than covert control, but you want it to appear to the dog that you are helping, not forcing, its behavior. You will not have to use the leash in this way for long.

❧ As soon as the dog is on the ground, turn to your right and with the dog at your left side, walk around in a semicircle so that the dog is once again lined up facing the front of the bench.

❧ Say the word "climb," and pull the dog up onto the bench. Then make eye contact, feed and praise the dog, and release it to jump down off the back of the bench by saying the word "free." If it is still necessary, pull the leash gently but firmly to get the dog off the bench.

Climb the beginning dog five times a session, with breaks of play in between, for a total of fifteen climbs in a day. It won't be long until the dog readily jumps on and off the bench by itself, thereby "escaping" all pressure created by your pulling on the leash. At that point you can begin increasing the number of climbs per session until you reach 25 to 30 climbs a day for the more experienced, and now more confident, dog.

Until the dog climbs on and off the bench on its own, you can either end the training session early or you can use the remaining two to three minutes to reinforce the named behaviors on the ground. It is also a good idea to do some low-stress eye contact at the end of the session.

In either case, end the training session, as always, with some extended eye contact, pets, and a little playtime. This is vital to keep the dog's mood up and its attitude to training positive.

Once the dog has learned to "escape" onto the bench, you can begin working on the stays. With my method, the word "stay" is unnecessary, and you should not bother the dog with trying to learn the word and what it implies. Once the dog happily jumps onto the bench to receive a food reward, you simply keep it on the bench for longer periods of time and reward it plentifully for being there, as follows:

❧ Stand beside the bench and feed the dog, with eye contact, every ten seconds.

- Then feed with eye contact every twenty seconds.
- Now feed it every thirty seconds, and so on.
- Over several sessions, gradually increase the length of time until the dog is staying on the bench for a full five minutes.

Of course, five minutes on the bench should earn the dog a truly generous amount of food treats, as well as lots of pets and praise. Don't be stingy with the food or the affection.

If the dog tries to get off the bench before you say "free":

- Restrain it gently but firmly with the leash.
- Say "ah–ah!" This is your mild admonition, and it should be used to effect here.
- Immediately make eye contact after any admonition by saying "yes," and give a food treat as soon as the dog settles back on the bench.

You will get two benefits from this. First, the dog will learn to stay on the bench until you release it with the word "free." Second, "ah–ah!" will become the only admonishment you will ever need to warn the dog off from an undesirable behavior.

When the dog can stay on the bench solidly for five minutes, you should begin to introduce distractions such as moving around and away from the bench, throwing a ball, or letting a cat or another dog walk by. Return to the bench and the dog's side regularly during this work to make eye contact and feed the dog generously. Let the dog assume any posture it wishes. It may sit, stand, or lie down, so long as it does not come down off the bench until you give the "free" signal. The dog will learn to understand the concept of the stay without having to learn the word. Be prepared to restrain the dog, using the leash gently but with firm, steady pressure, if it should try to leave the bench before you say "free."

The final test of this stage of training is to pull on the dog's leash and try to get it off the bench without giving the signal word "free." If the dog resists your attempts to pull it off, you know that the bench has now become a safe place where the dog has learned that staying is not an abstention from activity but rather an active behavior in which it engages willingly to earn reward and escape compulsion. Continue to work the stay on the bench, and over time increase it to twenty minutes.

Return to the bench and reward your dog for holding the stay. Here, Rhime shows a tight and compact sit, a nice side benefit of bench training.

Dogs trained with my method will happily jump up on a bench without any signal being given at all. This reflects the positive association they have formed with the exercise.

When you reach this point in training, pay special attention, as Chapter 4 discussed, to the importance of releasing the dog from work, so that it does not get locked into a trained behavior in which it has learned to feel safe. Staying in the escape behavior too long can create its own stress.

When your dog happily jumps on and off the bench on signal, you're ready for the next step: training the named behaviors on the bench.

Training Behaviors on the Bench

After you have the dog committed to the bench and the safety it finds there, you can use the bench to train the sit, stand, down, and the accompanying stays. If you have used the clicker, your dog should already know the names of the behaviors and how to give them. Do not be surprised, however, if the dog will not readily give the behaviors on the bench even though it has learned them with the clicker. This is normal and reflects the inherent unreliability of operant conditioning when it is not combined with other techniques.

In training the sit, stand, and down on the bench, you should always work all three behaviors in the same session. This is because training for three behaviors forces the dog to listen carefully to all signals. When only two behaviors are trained, the dog tends to "option" between the two. If it is sitting, it will down at the sound of your voice, and vice versa, rather than pay attention to what has been said. Stays, once again, do not need a signal word; the dog will learn to stay in the sit, stand, or down until you say the word "free" or give the next signal.

The Sit on the Bench

THE FIRST BEHAVIOR to train is the sit. Although you use your hands to position the dog, you should never push down on the dog's rear. Instead:

- Say the word "sit" while gently lifting up on the dog's chest with one hand and tucking the dog's rear end down under itself with the other hand. The dog will probably stiffen for a moment, then hang suspended briefly and slowly sink into the sit.
- When the dog's rear touches the bench, say the word "yes" to cause it to make eye contact and give a treat and praise.

The correct position to produce the "sit": your right hand is on the dog's chest to lift its front. Your left hand is tucking the dog's rear under itself (not pushing down on the dog's rear).

The Down on the Bench

FROM THE SIT you move the dog into the down, as follows:

- ❧ Take the leash in your right hand and with the same hand hold a piece of food in front of the dog's nose.
- ❧ Place your left hand behind the dog's withers (the shoulder blades).
- ❧ Say the word "down" and then begin to make a rocking motion by alternating pressure downward on the leash and on the withers.
- ❧ Do this rapidly, alternating pressure quickly from one hand to the other like pistons going up and down in sequence.
- ❧ When the dog resists pressure from the leash, push on the withers. When the dog resists pressure on the withers, pull down on

Step 1: In preparation for the down, hold the leash in your right hand, which also should hold a piece of bait. (Your dog will focus on the bait.) Place your left hand just behind the dog's withers. From this position you are ready to "seesaw" the dog down by alternating pressure on the leash and the dog's withers.

Step 2: Once your dog is down and tightly tucked, your leash should be loose and your hand will rest lightly on your dog's withers.

Let the Dog Decide

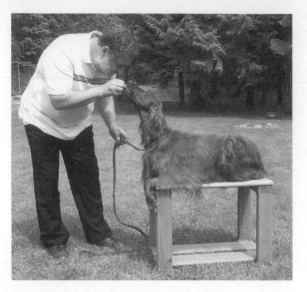

Step 3: You must raise your dog's head and not allow it to look at the ground. You can do this by feeding and making eye contact. This also dissipates any concern or stress that this procedure might have created in your dog.

the leash. Alternating rapidly between these pressures will give the dog nothing to resist against, and it will quickly go down.

* Once the dog's elbows hit the bench, say "yes" to get eye contact, and give food, pets, and praise.
* Next, move the dog back to the sit by saying the word "sit" and popping up on the leash.
* Do not pull up on the leash. Just keep popping it lightly until the dog sits up to stop the popping.
* When the dog sits up, say "yes" to make eye contact, and give food, pets, and praise.

The Stand on the Bench

TO MOVE THE dog from the down to the stand, position yourself at the dog's right side and do the following:

* Take the leash in your right hand and with the same hand hold a piece of food under the dog's nose, as you did for the down.
* Stand beside the dog so that you can reach both its head and its side. Say the word "stand" and move the bait forward away from the dog's nose while putting slight pressure on the flat collar with the leash with one hand and at the same time

Step 1: In preparation for the "stand," use food to maintain eye contact and to keep your dog's head up.

Step 2: With both the leash and a treat in your right hand, draw the dog forward into the stand.

Step 3: With your left hand, "tickle" your dog's loin, causing it to straighten its hind legs and assume the standing position.

tickling the dog in the loins with the other hand. Continue this until the dog stands.

❧ When the dog stands, say the word "yes" to attain eye contact and then give food, pets, and praise as before.

Repeat these exercises "hands on" until the dog begins to attempt to escape the indignity of being put in place. What you will notice is

Step 1: When preparing for the sit from the down, bait your dog with a treat to prevent it from dropping its head.

Step 2: Continue to offer the treat while popping up on the leash to bait your dog into the sit.

Step 3: When your dog is up and in the sit, keep its attention with treats and eye contact. Note the loose leash.

that the dog will begin to anticipate your actions and try to beat, or race, you to the behavior in an attempt to keep your hands off of it. Reward these attempts to "escape" by not touching the dog but only giving the signal word followed by eye contact, food, pets, and praise.

Make it clear, however, that any behavior that is given slowly or reluctantly brings your hands into play. In this way the fastest responses are rewarded and the slower responses are met with compulsion. I cannot say enough here about the importance of getting and maintaining

Lots of treats will help keep your dog's head up and will help maintain deep eye contact while working on the bench

eye contact with the dog. The dog will attempt other forms of escape from the pressure you are applying, but it must find only one safe harbor: compliance with the behavior you have signaled for.

If the dog attempts to drop its head, look at the ground, look past you, and so on, you must not allow this to happen. Be patient and feed and praise the dog heavily for eye contact at every opportunity. I might also mention here that the bench offers many opportunities to pet, praise, and "coo" to the dog in loving tones. Do not fail to take advantage of every chance to give the dog pleasure and affection for complying with your wishes.

Stays on the Bench in the Named Behaviors

WHEN THE DOG is giving the sit, stand, and down on the bench purely in response to the signal words, with no hands-on pressure from you, you can teach it to stay in these behaviors until signaled otherwise. Give the dog the signal to "sit," for example, and then move about the bench

Once your dog has learned not to leave the bench, you can begin to move about and train at a distance.

and create distractions. You can also pull on the leash as in the first training of the stay on the bench to test the dog's commitment to remaining in the signaled behavior until another signal has been given.

If the dog moves or changes behavior, admonish it with an "ah–ah!" and immediately put it back into the proper position with your hands. As soon as the dog is back in position, say the word "yes" to initiate eye contact and give food, pets, and praise.

When the dog has learned to escape any compulsion from the leash or your hands by giving the sit, stand, and down on the bench in response to the signal words, you can begin to pull on the dog with the leash to heighten the reliability of training. These pulls on the leash without you

Here are two bench-trained dogs (Greta and Penny) that understand not to move until they hear the word "free." These two dogs are "traffic-safe." Even though the van and crate doors are open, they will not move without permission.

giving a signal word will make the dog uncomfortable, as you are attempting to make it break a rule. The dog will resist this as much as it can, and the exercise will further develop its resistance to breaking the rules. The result will be that the dog will never change a signaled behavior until it hears the release word "free" or the next signal word.

You can also try to distract the dog by making your movements around the bench more animated and attractive to it. If your distraction makes the dog move out of a behavior before you have given the proper signal word, whether it is "sit," "stand," "down," or "free," immediately say, "ah–ah!" to admonish the dog and if necessary put the dog back into position with your hands.

This distraction work builds a psychological picture within the dog, where the signal you give is more important than anything else you do. Every dog owner knows how important this is, as every dog wishes to interpret the owner's movement as an excuse to move itself, especially during the teaching of the stays. The dog that will stay even in the face of pressure from its owner, however, is a reliable dog indeed.

You should also put more distance between yourself and the bench, even to the point of going out of sight for periods of time. I like to step around a nearby corner so I am out of sight but close enough to rush in if the dog attempts to move. The dog should become comfortable giving the sit, stand, and down when you give the signals from ten feet away.

Finally, you should work on extending the time the dog stays in the signaled behavior. Over several sessions, gradually build up to five minutes for the sit, one minute for the stand, and five minutes for the down.

To close this chapter, let me tell you about some very nice clients of mine, an English couple, who owned a lovely young Springer Spaniel they wanted to take hunting. They were not experienced in handling dogs, and I gave them a few days' guidance. After some weeks of training on their own, they asked me to stop by one day so they could show me something. I went over and they benched the dog in a stand. We went into the house and had tea and cookies. When we came back out twenty minutes later, the dog was still standing in the same position on the bench. This dog became an extremely reliable and steady hunter in the field.

I mention this to encourage you with the fact that you don't have to be a professional trainer to get results this impressive by using my methods. Be patient and cheerful with yourself and the dog, and you'll be amazed how fast the dog develops.

Intermediate Training on the Ground

Once the dog sits, stands, and downs on the bench when you give the signals from ten feet away, it is time to resume training on the ground. But don't throw away the bench. Like eye contact, the bench is a valuable tool that you will use over and over again before training is complete. Keep the bench nearby and ready to use. You may well find that the dog has become so fond of the bench, however, that you have to tip it over on its side to keep the dog from climbing on it.

Remember that each phase of training represents a new beginning for you and the dog and that it is important not to have unreasonable expectations of the dog's performance. I generally expect the dog to have difficulty and respond incorrectly at first on moving to ground work after the bench. This is normal.

This is not to say that your dog might not leap to the ground and do everything perfectly. That happens, too. Just be ready to help the dog out when you first make the change, especially by keeping your own mood positive and showing the dog an encouraging demeanor.

Also remember that it is important to show the dog a positive mood throughout training. But as I explained in Chapter 10, the bench is a relatively intimate classroom, so to speak, in which you show the dog a calm demeanor and gentle the dog between behaviors. In moving to phase three training on the ground, you should become more animated and establish a more casual, playful mood. The contrast between the bench and ground work will be a great asset as training progresses to completion.

Use your long line at all times during this phase of training. And for the first sessions, as described in the next section, run both a line and a leash on the dog.

You can return to using your clicker to encourage the correct responses in the first few sessions, but limit its use to helping the dog refresh the positive associations that were created during the teaching phase with the clicker. Then dispense with the clicker as quickly as possible.

Beginning to Train on the Ground

BEGIN THE FIRST sessions of intermediate training on the ground by attaching the leash and long line to the dog's flat collar. Later you will make a show of removing the leash, which will make the dog believe it is free from control and can do as it wishes, but you will leave the long line on for covert control. This will be an important step on the way to freeing yourself and the dog from leash-dependent training.

For now, keep both the leash and the long line on the dog, and:

- ❧ Take the leash in your hand and begin to walk about your training area slowly and casually, keeping the leash loose.
- ❧ Say the word "yes" at random to elicit eye contact from the dog.
- ❧ When the dog looks at you, drop food from your mouth for it to catch in its own mouth. At this stage, the dog should be well used to catching dropped food in its mouth.
- ❧ If the dog fails to catch the treat in the air, use the leash to keep it from picking the food off the ground. Pick the food up yourself, say "yes" to reestablish eye contact, hold the food close to your face, and then drop it for the dog to catch in its mouth. (My method asks that you put only clean human food treats for the dog in your own mouth, but there is no need to waste food that has fallen on the ground, either.)

This practice causes the dog to become intensely focused on your face. Follow this rule whenever the dog is close enough to you to catch food in its mouth, for example, when it is in the "front" position or at your side in the heel position. From now on in training, when you are rewarding a sit, stand, or down, approach the dog during eye contact so that the catch is fairly easy to make. You don't want to make it difficult for the dog to catch the food. You want the dog to succeed quickly, without frustration.

Sometimes you will still want to reward the dog when it is too far away to drop food from your mouth for it to catch in its own. In those cases, get eye contact and then throw the food away from the dog the same way you did while using the clicker, remembering to say "free" to release the dog to pick up the treat.

Try drawing the dog into the "front" recall position occasionally by using only the dog's name. It may seem odd to recall the dog to you when it is only six feet away from you at the other end of the leash. However, as I've said before, great recalls are built on this close work, and the recall is one of the most important behaviors for the dog to learn.

If the dog does not look up at you to make eye contact when it is in the "front" position, say "yes" to get eye contact and then drop the food to the dog to catch in its mouth. If the dog doesn't catch the food, remember not to let it get the food from the ground. Pick the food up yourself, say "yes" to reestablish eye contact, then drop the food again for the dog to catch in its mouth.

You can use the leash here to help get the dog into the front position if necessary, but you must do so surreptitiously. You must not drag or yank the dog into position. Here is the proper technique:

- Pass the leash between your legs and hold it behind your back.
- Pop backward on the leash, just firmly enough to make the dog begin to move forward.
- Continue popping until the dog is in a good "front" position.
- Say "yes" to make good eye contact, and feed the dog by dropping food from your mouth.
- Keep the dog in the front and continue to make it comfortable through eye contact and feeding.
- Release the dog with the word "free" when you are done.
- Casually walk about the training area once again, saying "yes" and dropping food from your mouth on eye contact, and recalling the dog by name to eye contact and food reward in the front position. Do this in a random sequence alternating with pure play.

The leash should be between your legs, but your dog should not be too far from you.

You can pop the leash covertly behind your back to help your dog begin to move forward into the correct position.

Continue this process through several sessions until the dog gives you its complete attention as you walk casually about the training area.

Building Reliability by Delighting the Dog

ONCE YOU HAVE the dog's complete attention, you will give the first formal signal. Choose whatever behavior the dog does best and likes the most—the sit, for example. When the dog gives the behavior in response to the signal, say "yes" and make eye contact.

Now say "free," throw several treats, and do a dance of joy with the dog. Never miss a good opportunity to do the spontaneous dance of joy in response to the dog's successful behavior. Remember that these silly, fun-filled moments intensify the dog's learning. Scientifically speaking, strong emotions lock in memories and give them a permanent mood. By behaving in a way that delights the dog, you ensure that it forms the most positive associations possible with the training behaviors and with you. This builds amazing reliability in the dog, and an amazingly strong bond with you.

Creating this extraordinary event—the dance of joy—indelibly marks in the dog's mind the importance you place on the successful behavior. The dog will never forget how you rewarded its first decision to comply of its own free will, when it felt free to refuse. For this reason, you must shower the dog with affection and reward. Be as playful as you can. Act like a puppy! Jump up and run a few steps in the manner of dogs playing with one another, then stoop down low to the ground and engage in more physical contact. The more you delight the dog, the deeper the effect will be. A dance of joy after the dog's successful behavior is also the best way to end a training session, particularly with a young dog or puppy.

Start the next several sessions the same way, by asking for the dog's most successful behavior and rewarding the behavior when the dog gives it. Then ask for another trained behavior, and with each succeeding session, add more and more formal behaviors to the mix. There should be no pattern to the sequence, which should be varied and random. The dog should never be able to anticipate which behavior you will ask for next.

Over the course of the training sessions, however, you should ask for an increasing number of downs, until they represent 50 percent of all signaled behaviors. You want the down more than anything else because it is the control behavior, the maximal position of safety for the dog and you. A dog that will go down and stay down cannot do anything wrong. And while the dog is in the down, you can quickly go over and put the leash on in times of trouble.

At this stage of training, never make the dog down, sit, or stand for more than a second or two. You are looking for the dog to give the behavior, not stay in it. Releasing the dog from the behavior quickly helps to build a positive attitude toward obedience.

Work the sit, stand, and down with the dog right in front of you, as on the bench. Anytime you can get the dog to sit, stand, and down while not directly in front of you is a bonus.

I always end sessions with the down, and I do the dance of joy with the dog for the down more than for any other behavior. Reward should be varied during this work. For example, a single piece of hot dog or cheese is sufficient for most behaviors, but two, three, four, and even five treats at a time not only mark the dog's best responses but keep its interest high. A typical routine goes like this:

☘ Signal for the sit (by this point, you should be training only with word signals, not the clicker). When the dog sits, say "yes" to elicit eye contact. And then say "free" and throw the treat away from the dog so that it must move to get it.

- Walk a few steps and signal for the down. When the dog downs, say "yes" to elicit eye contact. And then say "free" and throw the food.
- Walk a few steps and signal for the stand. Say "free" and release the dog.
- Now walk a few steps and call the dog into the "front."
- When the dog is in "front" position looking up at you, say "yes" to elicit eye contact. Then say "free" and drop a treat from your mouth. Remember that in this case the dog must catch the food. If the dog doesn't catch the food, do not let it get the food from the ground. Pick the food up yourself, say "yes" to reestablish eye contact, hold the food close to your face, and then drop it for the dog to catch in its mouth.
- Walk a few steps and signal for the "down," and so on for five minutes, interspersed with dances of joy for especially successful behaviors.
- End the session on another successful down, followed by a highly rewarding dance of joy including plenty of treats, pets, and praise.

What To Do If the Dog Balks

IF THE DOG refuses or fails to give a behavior on signal, take it straight to the bench. Climb the dog onto the bench and begin the routine with your leash well in evidence. You can leave the long line on the dog or drop it on the ground beside the bench if you find it inconvenient or awkward to do the bench work while the dog is wearing the long line. Just be sure to reattach the long line before you free the dog from the bench and take it back to the ground. Put your hands on the dog and compel it to assume the correct positions, no matter how well the dog did the exercises on the bench before you moved to the ground or how well it does them now. (See Chapter 11 to review using your hands to compel the dog.)

It is important to do this in a workmanlike, neutral manner, being sure to get eye contact for every behavior to prevent any attempt by the dog to slip into a defensive posture. Give friendly praise and treats when the dog races to get into position before you can compel it to do so with your hands, but do not be lavish with either. Keep your responses low-key and neutral. This is a piece of work that should be done quickly and efficiently.

Pay careful attention to how you are feeling and the mood you are showing the dog. You should not be disappointed or frustrated by having to go back to the bench. The dog's decision not to give a behavior now and then, especially early on in a training phase, is a normal part of its learning process and represents the opportunity to clarify for the dog what the winning response is. You are not punishing or disciplining the dog by putting it on the bench. You are giving it another opportunity to learn how to escape into safety, comfort, and reward.

When this is done:

- ❖ Take the dog back to the ground on the leash and long line. Dial your mood up a bit, so to speak, and adopt the somewhat more animated tone we discussed at the beginning of the chapter.
- ❖ Give the dog the signal for the behavior it failed to give earlier, and be ready to shower the dog with reward and affection—including the dance of joy—if it gives the behavior. End the session right there, with an extended dance of joy with and for the dog.
- ❖ If the dog fails once again to give the signaled behavior—this is a normal occurrence with some dogs—return to the bench and repeat the process of showing the dog the routine on the bench and reestablishing the behaviors in a relatively neutral yet still friendly way. Then go back to the ground to see if the dog is ready to give the behavior.
- ❖ Continue to repeat the cycle until the dog gives the missing behavior on the ground. As soon as the dog gives the behavior on the ground, shower it with all the enthusiasm, praise, pets, and treats you can muster, ending the session with the exuberant dance of delight for the dog.

These situations, where the dog refuses or fails to give a behavior and then decides to comply, are when doing the dance of joy is most effective. The contrast for the dog between being taken back to the bench or having you delight it will make its successful performance stand out dramatically in its mind. Under these circumstances the dog will readily choose compliance over the alternative.

Working without the Leash

WHEN THIS EXERCISE is going well and the dog readily gives the sit, stand, and down on the ground and comes to the "front" recall position without hesitation, start to take the leash off occasionally and work only with the long line in place. Make a grand gesture of removing the leash and saying "free," abandoning overt control in the dog's eyes while still maintaining covert control with the long line.

Removing the leash will free your dog for covert control with the long line.

The dog now believes it is free.

After you release the dog with the word "free":

- ❧ Turn your back to the dog and begin to walk away.
- ❧ When the dog begins to follow, reward it with praise.
- ❧ If the dog comes to your right side, reward it with more praise and a pet.
- ❧ If the dog comes to your left side, drop food from your mouth to the dog to catch and then give more lavish praise and pets.

The dog will soon decide that your left side—the heel position—is the one that has the most positive value.

From there, work the sit, stand, and down off the leash, remembering to do downs about half the time. If the dog takes advantage of its apparent freedom from your control to refuse a behavior or wander off on its own agenda during this exercise or the training sessions that follow, don't take this as a failure. It is a wonderful opportunity to use the long line to demonstrate to the dog that the area of your influence is not limited to the length of the leash but is virtually infinite. This is one of the most powerful learning experiences the dog can have.

If the dog refuses to heed a signal or wanders away on the long line:

- ❧ Immediately adopt neutral body language and say nothing to the dog.
- ❧ Step on the long line and "tightrope walk" down it about a third of its length.
- ❧ Crouch down low, turn sideways to the dog, look away, and call the dog to you in a very upbeat, encouraging tone.
- ❧ When the dog comes to you, say "yes," make good eye contact, and enthusiastically praise and reward the recall.
- ❧ Leash the dog and take it to the bench for a quick session there, again focusing on the behavior the dog failed to give.

"Tightroping" up the long line to the dog, who has refused to return with the ball.

Let the Dog Decide

The Stays

WHEN THESE LONG-LINE sessions are going smoothly and the dog is giving every behavior without hesitation, it is time to work on the stays. If you are not regularly taking the leash off during training sessions, you should make a point of doing so now.

Continue to use your long line on the dog at all times during training, however, so that you always maintain covert control.

Don't Lean on the Leash

THE LEASH IS a crutch that creates a strong dependence in you. No dog can fail to recognize this weakness in your handling and take advantage when the leash is no longer present.

Dispensing with the leash during training does not mean doing without it when you take the dog out in public. Always have your dog on the leash in public, unless you are in a dog park. This is for safety's sake, because you have no control over the vagaries of the world or the behavior of other people or their dogs. During training sessions, keep the leash in your pocket or easily accessible nearby.

Train the stays for the sit, stand, and down by leaving the dog in each behavior for an increasing length of time. Begin this exercise by keeping the dog in the stay for around five to ten seconds until you say "free." As the dog gains confidence and seems more relaxed, increase the time until the dog can easily stay in the sit for one minute, the stand for thirty seconds, and the down for two minutes.

This may take one session or many sessions, depending on the dog. Keep in mind that the number of sessions a dog needs to learn something does not necessarily indicate anything about its level of intelligence.

The length of time that the dog is held in the stay must be varied to prevent boredom and resentment. Try to work comfortably within the dog's increasing limits. When a dog gives you a five-minute stay for the first time, for example, you cannot then immediately expect the dog to hold every stay that long. That would be like asking a figure skater who had finally landed his first quadruple toe loop in a practice session to land it consistently in competition without ever practicing it again.

What you ask for regularly during training, and reward regularly when the dog gives it, is a performance that is well within its limits. Remember that learning is a stressful experience and that you cannot always expect the dog to give a peak performance. The number one key for good training is to keep the dog's conscious experience of stress low and its mood positive.

If the dog's longest stay is a minute, therefore, release the dog regularly after five or ten seconds. If the dog's longest stay is a couple of minutes, release the dog regularly after twenty or thirty seconds. If the dog's longest stay is five minutes or longer, release the dog regularly after no more than two or three minutes, and sometimes after only twenty or thirty seconds, and so on. It is even helpful to release the dog immediately when it most expects that you are going to want a long stay. Your unpredictability keeps the dog alert and helps build a positive mood toward the stays. The dog should never be able to anticipate when a stay is coming or how long the stay will be.

By this point in training the dog should be looking at you, if not making direct eye contact, every time you give it a signal. If this is not happening, say "yes" now and then to hold and strengthen eye contact while the dog waits. You can also approach and drop food to the dog to catch in its mouth. But do not say "free" until you are ready to release the dog from its position.

Never let the dog move from its position unless you have said "free." If the dog starts to move:

- ❧ Admonish it with an "ah–ah!"
- ❧ Turn square to the dog and lean in toward it a little. You aren't trying to threaten the dog but to warn it that it is getting out of reward position. The dog will remember this verbal admonition and warning body language from bench work.
- ❧ The instant the dog responds to this forceful tone and body language, change to more neutral body language, praise the dog in a mild, gentle tone, and keep it in position for another thirty seconds.
- ❧ Then release the dog to high reward by saying "free" and giving lots of praise, pets, and treats.

The dog soon learns that returning to the desired behavior and staying there makes you very pleased and that your response is always more rewarding than moving before you say "free."

If the dog does not return to the signaled behavior but rather "breaks" the stay, put the leash on and go back to the bench for a "hands on" session as described in Chapter 11. Remember to give particular attention to the behavior the dog did not stay in. Make the last behavior you ask for the one the dog "broke" on the ground, and have it do a stay on the bench in this behavior.

Now take the dog back to the ground and ask for the same behavior. If the dog gives and holds the position, shower it with reward and affection. Do the dance of joy to reward and mark the dog's decision to comply, thereby encouraging the dog to make the same decision the next time.

Remember that you have the long line on the dog and any refusal can be easily countered by walking tightrope down the line to the dog, putting the leash back on, and returning to the bench. Any and all attempts by the dog to avoid being controlled will be thwarted by the line while you calmly and casually approach. The dog will soon stop trying to "escape" in any way other than through compliance.

Once again, you must pay extra close attention to your own mood and demeanor in these moments of correcting the dog's behavior. Never show frustration or express anger in any way, verbally or nonverbally. Never punish or scold the dog. Your focus must be that of a good coach, setting the dog up to win, so that you can shower it with reward and affection. The good coach is firm and fair and by acting that way earns deference and respect. This is the most compelling argument to the dog to cooperate with you and give the proper behavior on signal.

13

Training Behaviors under Distraction

After the dog has progressed to giving all the behaviors on signal and coming in nicely to the front, as well as making good eye contact in all situations, you need to remember that the dog makes associations to behavior through specific circumstances. Every detail of these circumstances has a part in the dog's associations.

This fact explains why formal leash training fails so often in the real world. The dog makes associations to sitting, for example, because you always ask it to sit when it is on the leash directly in front of you or at your side in the heel position. In such circumstances, the dog doesn't have to understand the signal; it can give a rote response based on what usually happens when it is in the same position, including such details as the presence or absence of a leash, your body language, and so on.

Reliability in training requires that you progress to giving the dog all the different signals in all sorts of different situations. The first and easiest thing to vary is your own physical position relative to the dog. Move about at random and create every possible angle and distance to the dog. Give the signals when the dog is in front of you, beside you, and behind you, and at increasing distances from very close to five, ten, and thirty feet away.

The dog will want to move toward you when it hears the signal in an attempt to maintain its safety—closer is safer—and because of the associations that it has made on the bench and with the clicker. If the dog does this, you can practice with the dog "back tied," that is, with its leash or the long line attached to something behind it, so that it cannot approach you. Or you can surreptitiously loop the long line around a tree or a pole, like a mountaineer on belay.

During obedience training, you can "back tie" your dog (for example, by attaching the leash to a fence) to prevent your dog from approaching you.

A long line looped through the fence offers more apparent freedom to your dog; however, your dog still cannot approach you during training.

Vary the timing and sequence of the signals. Give several signals in a row in machine-gun fashion, for instance, then no signal for several moments followed by a few signals out of the blue, spaced ten to twenty seconds or so apart. Vary the speed and direction of your movement, including sitting and lying down on the ground.

When I see the dog consolidating its learning and becoming more consistent in its responses to signals in varied contexts, I like to stand with my face against a wall and give signals. This way I know that I am not inadvertently giving any body language clues to the dog. If the dog can rely on your body language to interpret what you want, it will never learn the right associations with the word signals. It will "listen" only by "looking." (For more on this problem, see Chapter 5.)

Work the stays in the same manner. Put the dog in a down, for example, and move about in relation to the dog. Walk away from and toward the dog quickly and slowly; move out of sight; run, jump up and down, lie on the ground; and so on. Keep your mood upbeat and encouraging, and reward the dog's best responses with lots of pets, praise, and treats.

You should now also begin to vary the schedule of reinforcement to the dog. Select only the dog's best responses for attention, or those given despite the highest levels of distraction. Get three or four behaviors before feeding. Never allow the dog to anticipate when the reward is coming or what the reward will be. Sometimes it should just be a small piece of hot dog; other times it should be a handful of something special. (I like to keep the fatty cuttings from pork chops or steaks for this purpose.)

When this starts to work well with the dog, it is time to introduce even higher levels of distraction. Now is when I bring out the dreaded cat or the annoying puppy and add them to the mix. Children are good, too, especially if they are running around screaming like banshees! If this work is done properly, the dog will generalize from these specific distractions to others it has not yet encountered.

If the dog has trouble on the ground with these distractions, put it back on the bench for a few sessions with the same distractions. I have cured many dogs of chasing cats by using the bench.

The Recall

THE RECALL IS the second most important behavior you will teach the dog, behind only the down (the "control" behavior). The first step includes recalls from no farther away than the end of a six-foot leash, because it is always best to train the last links in a behavioral chain first and work backward to the beginning. That way the dog always knows what comes next and stress is greatly reduced. For the same reason, I will do recalls from as close as six inches when I start training this behavior.

That's exactly the pattern you've been following in this book. Teaching the recall actually began when you first worked the "front" with benevolent eye contact and taught the dog to feel safe and enjoy catching food in that position. The next step was teaching the dog to come to the front position at random from very close to you, in response to hearing its name called. Now that the leash is no longer in evidence because you are using only the long line for covert control, you can begin to add length to the recall.

In training the recall you must follow one important rule: Never call the dog to you out of a down. Only call the dog when it has already been released with the word "free" and is engaged in some activity or from the sit or stand. The dog must always stay down until you walk up to the dog and release it by saying "free" or give it a new signal by saying "stand" or "sit" and putting the leash on the flat collar.

This is because the down is the "control" behavior, the "safety" position. When you put the dog into the down, it must not get up without permission. The association you want the dog to form is that it cannot move from the down until you arrive at its side and give it a new signal. This rule will keep the dog safe when there is good reason for it to stay still, such as when other dogs are fighting in the dog park or there is traffic nearby.

To train the recall:

❧ Put the dog into a sit, walk a few feet away, and call it to you by saying its name.

❧ You may bait the dog into the front position when it arrives, if need be, by luring it closer with a piece of food held between your fingers.

❧ Then drop food from your mouth for the dog to catch in its mouth.

❧ Keep the dog there for as many food drops as you can manage. If you can't hold more than one piece of food comfortably in your mouth, put each piece of food into your mouth separately

Prepare to recall your dog by standing on the long line.

During random recalls, change your angle and distance, making sure you have ready access to the long line if the dog refuses.

and drop it to the dog to catch in its mouth. Dropping food from your mouth is crucial to strengthening benevolent eye contact.

❧ When you have finished giving treats, pets, and praise, release the dog by saying "free."

Remember you have your long line on the dog in case the dog refuses to come. By this stage, that should happen only rarely. But if it does, immediately tightrope walk one-third of the way down the line, crouch down low, turn sideways, avert your eyes, and call the dog to you in the most encouraging way possible. When the dog arrives, put on the leash and practice short recalls to remind the dog of how safe and rewarding it is to be in the front.

Work the recall further and further from the dog, until you are at least thirty paces away when you call it to you by saying its name. Also vary the time you make the dog wait until you call its name. Be sure to shower the dog with pets and praise for good recalls once it has been fed a treat and eye contact is complete.

Introducing Distractions

NOW THAT THE dog is giving strong formal recalls at thirty paces, you can begin to introduce distractions. Allow the dog to become interested in the environment before calling it to you. Make a big fuss when the dog comes during the beginning stages of this exercise.

Although you should recall the dog in a random pattern, you should only do so when you can step on the long line easily if the dog fails to come to you. In that case once again tightrope walk down one-third of the line, crouch down low, and encourage the dog to you. Put the leash on the dog and practice recalls from short distances to remind the dog of the safety and comfort of the front. Once the dog is responding to the recall on the leash, you can go back to working only with the long line attached to the flat collar.

As you begin to see reliability in the recall, start to use the word "here" when you call the dog, as follows:

❧ Say the dog's name first followed by the "here"; for example, "Fluffy! Here!"

- ❧ Over the course of several more sessions, slowly drop the dog's name from the phrase and only use the word "here."
- ❧ Once this is working well, use the dog's name for informal recalls and "here" for formal recalls. This is to say that you will always have the dog come to the front position on the word "here" and just have it come close to you on hearing its name. (For an explanation of the need for formal and informal signals, see Chapter 5.)

THERE IS ONE more formal behavior to train: the heel.

The Heel

Chapter 6 explains how to train the dog to walk on the leash. The heel is something else altogether. It is a formal exercise that is a special test of the bond between dog and handler.

The heel is the most difficult of all the obedience exercises because it is simultaneously an abstention (not moving away from you) and an action (moving in harmony with you). When training this behavior, you must be endlessly patient with both the dog and yourself. Smart obedience competitors will take two to four months, or even longer, to train the heel to perfection.

Heeling in a Straight Line

To begin training the heel, you must teach the dog the transition from the front to the heel position. The dog should already be familiar with the heel position from your dropping food to it while it is at your side. The dog should also know that "yes" means to look at you.

With this foundation:

- ❧ Put the leash on the dog, and take the leash in your right hand, allowing the long line to drag on the ground behind you.
- ❧ Call the dog into the front position by saying "here." (Do not say the dog's name.)

Your dog should be in the front in preparation to move to the heel position.

While baiting your dog with a treat, step back with your left foot.

Your dog will now be beside you.

Move your left foot forward so that your feet are together and you have drawn your dog into the heel position. Feed your dog treats while making eye contact.

Once your dog sits in the heel position, reinforce the good behavior with treats and pets.

- Bait the dog by holding food in front of its nose with the left hand.
- Using the bait as a lure and the leash as a guide, step backward with your left foot and draw the dog into a position alongside of you.
- Continuing to use the bait as a lure and the leash as a guide, step forward with your left foot so that you are in your original position. The dog will turn to follow the bait and will now be standing at your side, facing forward.
- Say "sit," and when the dog sits, say "yes" and drop food to it to catch in its mouth.
- The dog is now in the heel position.

Do not name this behavior until the dog is doing it well. You may then call this signal "heel" or "fuss." (For information on choosing signal words, see "Formal and Informal Signals and Control" in Chapter 5.)

The next part is easy, as you have already encouraged the dog to choose to be at your left side during the random work you did when you first brought the dog off the bench.

- While the dog is sitting beside you and making eye contact, step forward very slowly and say the word "yes" to maintain eye contact.
- Take only the one step and say "free" and drop food to the dog to catch in its mouth.
- Give the dog a big display of your affection.
- Now return to the same spot where you began (it is not necessary to step backward and forward as in the preceding, "come to heel from the front" exercise again; you should work this exercise separately), and encourage the dog back into the heel position.
- Repeat this five or six times at each session and then move on to other work or end the session.

Once both you and the dog are comfortable with walking one step in the heel position, walk two steps before dropping food for the dog to catch in its mouth and saying "free." In the beginning you may allow the dog to pick up the food from the ground if it has difficulty catching while in motion. However, you should quickly progress to not

Drop treats to your dog while it is taking the first step out of the heel.

An example of moving away from overt control and leash dependence to off-leash heeling: the dog is heeling happily, and the leash is visible to the dog, but is no longer being used for overt control.

allowing the dog to collect food from the ground, just as during the initial phases of training for eye contact. Continue to add steps, always walking slowly, until you can take ten or so steps without the dog looking away from you.

Turning in the Heel Position

NOW YOU ARE ready for the first turn. You have taught the dog to watch your face and look into your eyes while walking beside you, and this will now become a convenient aid in showing the dog where you are going. If you turn your head in the direction of the turn, before you need to turn your body, the dog will grasp your intention and prepare to turn with you, thanks to its ability to interpret body language. For example, one step before a right turn, you turn your head to face in that direction.

Here is how to do it:

❧ With the dog sitting at your left side in the heel position, say "yes" and slowly walk forward six or seven steps, staying within the limit of the dog's attention span for the exercise so far.

❧ Prepare yourself and the dog for a right turn by turning your head quickly to the right one step before the turn. The dog should be alert to this and follow your gaze, because you have trained the dog to make and maintain eye contact.

❧ Turn to the right very slowly.

❧ Take one more step to complete turning the corner, say "free," and drop food to the dog to catch in its mouth. (Never feed the dog "in the corner." Only feed after the turn is made and you are both on a straight line again.)

Make sure you delight the dog for successfully completing this difficult maneuver. I love to romp with the dog after each repetition of this exercise and play my way back to the starting position to do it again.

You do exactly the same for the left turn, except that a step before the turn you quickly turn your head to the left to prepare the dog for the change in direction. And then slowly turn to the left, walking one more step to complete the corner before rewarding the dog.

Throughout this exercise you should walk very slowly. The dog will not make progress if you rush.

Notice that in the right turn you move away from the dog and therefore the dog "pursues" you through the corner. In the left turn you move toward the dog, and this could easily be misinterpreted as a threat. Give the dog plenty of time to figure out that the left turn of your head a step before the turn means that you are going to step in toward it, so that the dog has a chance to avoid a bump.

Do not bang the dog with your knee. Otherwise this contact will create an avoidance response in which the dog will swing wide of you to escape your knee.

Practice these turns both on and off leash, but always with the long line on the dog. When you do use the leash, do not jerk the dog around with it. Keep the leash loose and only use it as a guide, if you use it to direct the dog at all. At this stage the dog will be intent on keeping your face in sight and there should be no need to pull it with the leash.

If the dog is not intently trying to keep your face in sight, go back to the front position and make eye contact more appealing by rewarding the dog heavily. Also sit in a chair and feed the dog its favorite treats for making eye contact.

The Spinning Game

ONE OF THE games I like to play with the dog at this point in training, and before, is to turn about slowly in a spinning motion and spit food to the dog as it "chases" around me trying to keep eye contact. I spit the food for the dog's best effort and always give it a good chance to succeed, but over time I also make the game more challenging by gradually spinning faster and faster. With competition dogs I eventually whirl quite quickly, and the dog will pursue eye contact at an incredible speed. This is not a dog that is likely to be out of position during an obedience trial or on a normal walk.

You now know how to train all the formal obedience behaviors. If you keep each day's three formal five-minute training sessions upbeat, fun, and rewarding, and follow the guidelines for general handling and informal training during the rest of the day, your dog will achieve a supreme level of training.

NEXT, LET'S CONSIDER some special concerns that can arise in owning dogs.

• PART FOUR •

Special Concerns

15

Having More Than One Dog

Owners of more than one dog face very specific problems that
must be properly addressed, if the household is going to be a
happy one for dogs and people alike. First of all, you should never
acquire two dogs from the same litter. The special relationship that littermates have with each other often produces severe problems that not
even breeders and expert trainers handle well. The precise reasons for
this are not well understood, but animal behaviorists have established
that when littermates are raised together past eight weeks of age, they
arrest each other's development. It is as if the two animals are parts of
one dog and neither can be complete in itself.

Conclusive evidence for this phenomenon came from guide dog
training, as reported by Clarence Pfaffenberger in his landmark book,
The New Knowledge of Dog Behavior. Puppies selected for guide dog
training are placed with foster families that care for them and do the
basic training that prepares them to learn their guide duties. When a
guide dog group observed that certain foster families produced the best
guide dogs, they gave them littermates to raise. As you may imagine,
these were the most genetically appropriate dogs available. Yet when
littermates were fostered together, none of them could qualify as
guide dogs.

If you must have two dogs of the same breed, either go to different
breeders for each dog or choose from different litters when using the

With the right method, owning and handling multiple dogs can be fun.

same breeder. Life will be easier if you pick dogs of different sexes to live together. One male and one female to make up your pair will lessen the likelihood of fights and competition between your dogs. Males tend to be much more aggressive with other males, and likewise females are much more aggressive with other females.

Whether you want two dogs of the same or different breeds, you should try to make sure that the dogs have different temperaments. In particular, the greater the difference in the dogs' dominance characteristics, the fewer problems there will be.

Total attention and commitment from two high-drive working dogs.

The best combinations are a strong, confident, dominant male matched with a soft, easygoing female, or a strong, confident, dominant female with a soft, easygoing male. There is little reason for such dogs to be in conflict with one another, and any problems between them will be solved quickly and easily. If you are getting dogs of different sizes, life will also be more manageable if the smaller dog is the more excitable of the two. What you want to avoid at all costs are two dogs with the same status or who are too evenly matched in other ways.

A pair of troublemakers from the Hound group show that even they can live happily and cooperatively together.

Acquiring Two Dogs at the Same Time

IF YOU HAVE decided to get two puppies at the same time, you must provide them with separate crates, so that each of them has its own den, and train them separately. And although you will have them socializing together in your home, you must not let them interact freely with one another in their early days together.

The greatest threat in the multiple-dog household is that the dogs will find their primary relationship with each other rather than with the owner. The dogs then respond less and less to the owner, as the importance of their relationship to each other grows over time.

If you acquire two puppies, therefore, you must not let them become involved in prolonged interactions with each other, even apparently peaceful ones. Likewise, it must be you who arbitrates all disputes, not the dogs. Letting the dogs work things out between themselves, as if they were members of a wild pack, is a formula for disaster. They are not in the wild; they are now part of a human family and must act accordingly. The most important way in which you make this clear to the dogs is by stepping in whenever the dogs are in a dispute with each other.

In this regard, you must be aware of the fact that what you may think of as play fighting is actually a deadly serious contest to decide territory and status. This is not behavior you want your dogs to engage in at any time.

The sure sign that you should break up the dogs' interaction, whatever it may be, is when they have stopped looking up to you regularly for approval and reassurance. To handle these situations:

- ❧ Say "ah–ah" in a firm tone of voice.
- ❧ If the dogs are engaged in physical contact with each other, whether this seems playful or serious, you can separate them with the long lines before you say anything. Since the dogs are focused on one another in this instance, you can pick up the line of one dog and pop it out of the situation. If one of your dogs seems to consistently be the aggressor in these circumstances, you can put a line on only this dog.
- ❧ Standing erect with square shoulders, step in between the dogs. Say "ah–ah" again firmly if the dogs try to ignore you and reengage with each other.
- ❧ Put each dog in its crate for some quiet time.

Feed the dogs separately from one another so that the dog that finishes its meal first cannot approach the dog that is still eating. If you feed the dogs in their crates, it will prevent competition over food and also build each dog's positive association to the crate.

Also take the dogs out to toilet separately. You must be especially careful to pick up the dogs' stools promptly, because otherwise any parasite or illness in one dog will quickly spread to the other. Remember that even if you have only one dog, it is not healthy for anyone in the family, including the dog, for the dog's stool not to be picked up on a daily basis.

Finally, again, you must train each dog separately. When the dogs are each able to give the sit, stand, and down reliably on signal, work them through the same behaviors together to ensure that they will respond appropriately under the distraction of each other's presence. If one of the dogs fails to cooperate while you are working the two dogs together, there are several strategies you can use:

- ❧ If reliability is low because you are just beginning the groundwork, put the troublesome dog in a crate, where it can watch while you work the other dog for two to five minutes with lots of praise and reward.

❧ If reliability is higher, put the troublesome dog on the bench and work the other dog free on the ground.

❧ If the training level is higher still, put the troublesome dog in a down on the ground and keep it there while you work the other dog free.

❧ If both dogs seem troublesome but their individual reliability is high, put each in a down on its own bench and keep it there while you work them alternately.

Introducing a New Dog into an Established Single-Dog Household

THE MOST DIFFICULT transition in dog ownership is introducing a second dog into an established single-dog household. This must be done with great care and attention.

All the guidelines above about choosing puppies with different, complementary temperaments and other attributes, whether of the same or different breeds, apply to choosing a new dog to join your existing one. There is an additional wrinkle here, however: You must recognize that your first dog has territorial rights to both you and the home. The first dog may well be willing to use aggression to stop the process of integrating the second dog, who will almost certainly be seen as an interloper and a threat. Merely stopping any obvious aggression toward the new dog will not ensure peace and contentment over the long haul. Dogs are more than smart enough to wait until you are not present to make their feelings known, violently, to any intruder.

The trick here is to go slowly and carefully. Start by introducing the dogs to one another on neutral territory, which is to say, off your property. A trip to the park is a good idea. Have the existing house dog handled by the person it is most bonded to in the home. Make sure you have plenty of treats on hand, and be ready to reward the "home" dog for all friendly advances or responses to the new dog. Your goal is to create as positive an association as possible between the dogs.

If they are willing to play together, let them do so, but follow all the rules for visiting the dog park in Chapter 6 and for breaking up play fighting as described in the previous section. Wait until things are going well between the dogs, and then walk them home together. Try to spend some time in the yard or any other property surrounding the house before taking the dogs inside. Respect any territorial rights or favorite places your first dog may have developed in the home. Be careful not to do anything that might make the first dog jealous of the new dog. Once the dogs are in the home together, be sure to make yourself the center of their universe.

Above all, do not give the new dog attention while ignoring the first dog. Whenever you give the new dog pets, treats, and attention in the first dog's presence, you must also give the first dog a full share of the same. While you are giving the new dog attention, for example, have another member of the household give the first dog attention, and then trade places to take account of any especially possessive feelings the first dog may have about you or anyone else in the house. If you live alone, you may want to recruit a friend to help you out in such moments.

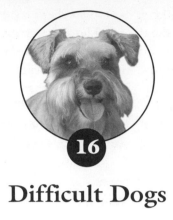

16

Difficult Dogs

There are four types of dog that are especially difficult to handle: the dominant dog, the active resister, the passive resister, and the fear biter (also known as the sharp-shy dog). There is hope for all, in most cases, except the fear biter.

These dogs may display similar behavioral problems for quite different reasons. The descriptions that follow will help you understand each of the four types. For information on solving specific behavior problems with these dogs or others, see Chapter 17.

Every characteristic of living creatures occurs on a continuum from less to more, mild to extreme. The mild to moderately dominant dog, active resister, and passive resister will all respond well to the training system in this book, assuming you begin training them as puppies. But puppies on the more extreme end of each type often require great efforts before effective training can begin. And with fear-biting, sharp-shy dogs, even the greatest efforts will almost always fail. In addition, the older a dog with a difficult profile is, the harder it will be to train, because its problematical behaviors will be all the more firmly established.

Keeping and training a dog that is strongly dominant or actively or passively resistant requires an equally strong commitment on your part. With that in mind, let's examine each of the four types.

The Dominant Dog

DESPITE THE CONTINUAL reference to dominance behavior in the literature of dog training, dominance in dogs is not well understood. This is particularly so when the social order involves both humans and dogs. What is clear is that variation is the key to Mother Nature's plan for all animals. Each litter of pups must provide diversity to the pack, which needs to have its leaders and followers—the strong and the weak, the bold and the shy—to survive.

The shy, nervous dog provides an early-warning system in the case of an attack. The bold, brave dog will take the necessary risks that bring success in the hunt and defense from predation and suffer the hard lessons of death and injury when it risks too much. The animals that represent the middle ground are the heart and soul of the pack, and also make the best pets.

One explanation that has been advanced for dominance is that it is the product of competition among littermates, with the strongest animals emerging as dominant. Another explanation, based on observation of play among littermates, is that dominance passes among the members of a litter, with each pup taking a turn. A third possible explanation, that dominance is formed in the womb, is based on the fact that some pups are treated with deference from birth not only by the other pups but by the mother as well.

From my own observations and experience, I believe that the third theory is correct and that dominant dogs are born dominant. Mother Nature makes her choices early and without reservation. Some must lead and others must follow, and both leaders and followers must assume their roles instinctively if the pack is to succeed.

Misunderstandings about dominance arise from the fact that behaviors we associate with dominance can appear in any dog if the circumstances are right. For example, the dog that is overly aggressive at the door with strangers sees the owner as weak and ineffectual for failing to respond to the threat represented by activity outside the door. The dog behaves as it does because the owner has not responded appropriately to this important circumstance. The dog is not expressing dominance but is acting to protect the owner, in the absence of a clear signal that the owner does not need protection. Any dog will do this.

Apparent dominance behavior also occurs when a dog seeks to protect its owner from other dogs. This can arise from two different misunderstandings. The first is that the owner has failed to read threatening behavior in another dog's actions. If I had a dime for every time I have heard an owner say, "Don't worry; my dog is friendly" as it approached me with its tail straight up in the air, walking on tiptoes, and its hackles clearly displayed, I'd be a rich man. All of these behaviors are very threatening, and no dog would fail to understand them.

The second possibility is that the dog is jealous and possessive because it does not see clearly that the owner loves it more than any other dog. This is not unlike the way children can become upset when their parents praise other children in their presence.

Many poorly trained dogs express total disdain for their owners' authority. Most of these dogs are the furthest thing from dominant. All dogs are looking to climb the status ladder just as surely as businesspeople wish to climb the corporate ladder. Both are looking to fill any vacuum that they discover above them. Dogs want access to resources and will do what it takes to ensure their piece of the pie. Who can blame them?

The dominant dog needs no special circumstances to provoke challenges or aggression. It responds to pain as a stimulus and resists any clumsy attempts at control. The dominant dog believes it owns the person, not the other way around.

Trying to be alpha pack leader over this dog invites a lifetime of conflict and endless challenges to your leadership. It also invites attacks or displays of aggression toward you, or toward members of the household or visitors that the dog sees as having lower status than you. The dog with a dominant temperament that has been "alpha trained" will never submit to anyone except the person it perceives as alpha, and it will continually test that person's authority.

To live happily with a dominant dog, you must make it your partner, not your rival for authority. Failure to understand this will lead to serious consequences. Of course, if you own a dominant dog, you must be able to control its behavior. It's the method of control that is important. You want such a dog to see you as an ally, helper, and friend, never as a competitor.

The dominant dog has many advantages as a working dog. Its desire to succeed produces endless streams of energy, and it will never quit when the going gets tough. The dominant dog's determination to win in every aspect of life makes it ideal for expert trainers who understand how to provide reward in exchange for deference. The dominant dog demands a great deal of work, and you must be prepared to do this work to own it. In return, you will have the best that dogs have to offer.

If you are looking solely for a pet and companion, however, it is best to stay away from the dominant dog, or indeed from any other extreme. The problem is in being able to recognize the extreme case in order to avoid it. This alone is reason enough to use a good breeder and purchase a purebred dog. If your breeder does not know which dogs are dominant in his or her own litters, it's time to find another breeder.

Characteristics of the Dominant Dog

EVEN AS A puppy, the dominant dog:

- ❧ Comes directly at you and pushes at you relentlessly.
- ❧ Walks up on its toes with its tail up in situations where it perceives a challenge.
- ❧ Has no difficulty staring you in the eye and does this on its own terms.
- ❧ Goes first through the door, before you or its littermates, and is first to the food bowl.
- ❧ Readily growls when you approach its food or possessions or when it has a stick, bone, or ball but seldom has its hackles (the hair on the shoulders and back of the neck) raised, as this is a sign of fearfulness and anxiety, feelings the dominant dog rarely experiences.
- ❧ Does not freely give up the ball when you play fetch.
- ❧ Pulls hard into the leash and insists on going its own way.
- ❧ Never gives an inch to any other dog and may be quick to fight when the opportunity arises.
- ❧ Is driven to win in all endeavors.
- ❧ Shows disdain for the weak and indifference or dominant aggression toward strangers and never sucks up to anyone.
- ❧ Will boldly stick its nose in your private parts to sniff you.

Assessing Dominance in Puppies

ONE OF MY favorite ways to test the confidence and status of a young dog is to lie on the ground face down and cover my head with my hands. The lower-status dog will frantically try to burrow under me and show considerable stress in the form of whining and submissive posturing at my behavior. Without a person standing above it, the lower-status dog feels naked to the world and anxious about being left in charge. The dominant puppy will stand on or over me, calmly accepting its superior position as natural.

Training the Dominant Dog

THE TRAINING METHODS in this book are just what the doctor ordered for the dominant dog. Make sure the dog wins at every turn, but only for deferring to you. It must sit and wait for permission to pass through every door. It must sit and ask for its food at every meal, and so on.

Consistency is crucial in training any dog, no matter what its temperament. But you must never break a rule for the dominant dog or give it the benefit of the doubt in any situation.

"Never let them see you sweat" must be your motto. You must remain calm, clear, and positive during training sessions, and your control over the dog must appear effortless. Constantly use the long lines covertly to control the dog's movement through the world. Interfere with its movement frequently, and wait until you see it let down or stop struggling against the long line before allowing it to approach its interests.

Reward the dominant dog's every look to you for help and comfort. If you must confront the dog, do it on your terms and when you are ready, not when it provokes you into a reaction. If the dog gives you trouble, put it up in the crate or kennel. Never engage in a conflict with the dominant dog if you are unprepared to finish it and come out on top. This is especially true if the dog ever displays aggression toward people, except in the context of being trained to display controlled aggression for protection work.

If the dominant dog shows inappropriate aggression, there are two ways to address the problem. The first requires that you respond to the aggression the instant it appears with overwhelming force; you must immediately and completely defeat the dog physically. Harsh as this method sounds, it will keep the dog from repeating its aggression and enable you to proceed with training.

A client of mine told me about facing this issue with a protection-trained German Shepherd import from Europe, before he began working with me. He was using a capable, old-school trainer who was accustomed to putting dogs into working situations rather than into people's homes as a pet and companion. Shortly after bringing the dog home, the client saw it move to attack one of his children.

Reacting instinctively to protect the child, the client grabbed the dog. They were at the top of a flight of stairs, the client stumbled, and the two of them tumbled down the stairs together, with the result that the client wound up on top of the dog. Both man and dog were bruised, and the dog had the wind knocked out of it. The immediacy and force of the blows the dog received in falling down the stairs and having a good-sized man land on top of it taught it an unforgettable, permanent lesson: It must never show aggression to the children again. It never did, and it became one of the best-loved pets the family ever had.

By lucky accident, the client had done exactly what was needed. But few people can respond in such cases in time and with appropriate force.

The second method, which does not risk harm to the dog or owner, and is one I employ, involves the Halti head collar. As Chapter 17 explains, the Halti collar is a painless means of controlling a dog's status and a great tool for any dog that is having trouble learning to walk properly on the leash. To use the Halti on the strongly dominant dog, first consult "Pulling on the Leash" in Chapter 17, then take the following steps:

- ❧ Make sure you can devote several hours a day to the problem for at least several days in a row. You may or may not need all this time, but once you begin to use the Halti, you cannot interrupt the process until it is complete.
- ❧ Wear sturdy clothes, including a long-sleeved jacket and blue jeans or heavy work pants.
- ❧ Put the Halti on the dog so that it fits very snugly and securely

and attach a stout leash. The dog must not be able to get the Halti off.

- ❧ When the dog fights the Halti, pull up on the leash so that the Halti closes the dog's mouth and the dog is unable to reach the leash with its paws. In frustration, the dominant dog will likely turn on you, thrashing and scratching at you with its legs and butting you with its head.
- ❧ If the dog rears up on its hind legs to flail at you with its front legs, step to the side, allowing the dog's front feet to fall back to the ground, then lift up on the Halti once more.
- ❧ This battle may go on for some time. While it rages, you must remain neutral and not show any anger or frustration toward the dog.
- ❧ When the dog exhausts itself, say nothing and casually lead it off on a friendly walk.
- ❧ The dog may try to ingratiate itself with you by nuzzling against you. Do not pay any great attention to this. Give the dog a little pet, and continue the walk. Then calmly praise the dog and put it in its crate or kennel.
- ❧ Repeat this procedure every day until the dog no longer fights the Halti.
- ❧ Continue to use the Halti to walk the dog, at least until its training is complete.

In these situations, you are not out to defeat the dog. Your goal is to show the dog that its strategy will never succeed. As soon as the dog realizes this, it will stop the unwanted behavior. Remember, dogs abandon behaviors that fail, and this is true for dominant dogs as well as meeker ones. Remember, too, that you cannot force any dog to give a reliable response. You must let the dominant dog decide to behave properly, and it will make that decision if you shape its training in a consistent, no-nonsense way.

Using the Halti brings the dog's status down in relation to you, and this is a bitter experience for the dominant dog. Training using the methods in this book balances things out for the dog by teaching it how to win through compliance. Once the dog sees how compliance produces reward, its dominance characteristics will pay off big-time and all its energy and drive will go into succeeding in training.

The Active Resister

DOGS THAT ARE active resisters may or may not have dominant temperaments. Whatever its dominance profile, such a dog resists all attempts to train or control its behavior. If you go right, it goes left. If you want up, it wants down. If you move in any direction, it pulls in the opposite.

The active resister worries endlessly at its collar, chews on the long and light lines no matter what you might do to deter the behavior, bites at the leash on walks, and pulls endlessly on its tie-out. It will not lie still or be calm when you wish it to be. When you put water down, the active resister spills it all over the floor. It refuses to go in the crate or get in or out of the car. It may bark constantly if it is contained or left alone.

Characteristics of the Active Resister

A DOG THAT is an active resister:

- ❧ Digs and chews and destroys things.
- ❧ Pushes the children around and steals their food and treats if it can, but it does not bite them. Instead, it may charge at those it sees as weak and slam into their legs and bodies with its own. In this "accidental" fashion, it may repeatedly knock down Grandma or old Aunt Florence.
- ❧ Does not come when called, no matter how you beg and plead. It dances maddeningly just out of hand's reach when you need to control it the most.
- ❧ Constantly paws at, jumps up on, and scratches at anyone who tries to train it.
- ❧ Will seldom growl or bite but may mouth the hand that seeks to control it.
- ❧ "Just won't listen." It is willful and disobedient in every aspect of life. The more upset and frustrated you get, the happier the dog seems to be.

Training the Active Resister

TAKE HEART. THE active resister responds wonderfully well to the training method in this book. What you must focus on is staying calm and relaxed in all situations. Let the system handle the dog for you.

Do not allow the frustrated, angry, desperate feelings the dog provokes in you to affect your behavior. Do not yell at the dog or threaten it. The dog's actions are not personal. It would do this to anyone who owned it. The active resister is the mischief maker of the dog world, but handled properly, it will become a great pet and companion. Patience and perseverance will win the day.

This situation calls for the crate more than any other. If your dog is an active resister, review Chapter 5's discussion of crate training. The crate is your best friend with this dog. The worst mistake you can make is to get the dog out of your hair by putting it out of the house into the backyard. The dog will simply have fun turning the yard into a moonscape.

If the dog barks and whines to excess in the crate, you may need to purchase a "no-bark" collar to prevent its noisemaking (there are both electronic and nonelectronic no-bark collars). But putting the crate into an unoccupied room or a closed garage should do the trick. And then perhaps put the radio or stereo on as well!

In any case, the dog must learn that it cannot access good things without your participation. It should be crated for twenty minutes before and after every training session. Training sessions must be highly rewarding, and in contrast there must be no treats or attention outside of the session itself.

Use the Halti head collar when you take the active resister on walks (see "Pulling on the Leash" in Chapter 17). Expect the dog to buck and fight like a wild horse to get the Halti off and to continue to do this for days. You must remain calm and unaffected by these demonstrations. Pay the dog no mind until it stops fighting the Halti, and then reward the dog with pets, praise, and treats. Do not expect to take this dog on a walk for any purpose but Halti training for some time.

Show nothing but complete indifference to the active resister's bad behavior, but be quick to reinforce its every attempt to be good. As with the dominant dog, make frequent, covert use of the long lines to frustrate the dog's ability to move about freely on its own agenda. You must be as secretive and sneaky as possible when doing this.

When you feel your frustration rising, put the dog in its crate, saying "good dog" as you do so. Keep long lines on the dog both inside and outside the house (see Chapter 5). As with all dogs, you must be able to catch the active resister without effort if it tries to avoid or escape from you and the training situation. Stand or step on the long line whenever you need to control the dog. After the active resister is back in its crate, you can go to another room and vent your frustration freely.

Be patient and stay with the program, and this hardheaded, stubborn mischief maker will become the best dog you are ever likely to own. The dog will turn every ounce of energy it used to resist you around to meet your every wish!

The Passive Resister

THE DOG THAT resists passively is a heartbreaker. It shivers and shakes continually and flinches at your every gesture in an attempt to duck a blow that has never been struck. When people see the passive resister, they often whisper or say out loud, "Oh! That poor dog has been beaten!" All of your protestations to the contrary will fall upon deaf ears.

Such a dog falls to the ground at the slightest application of pressure and rolls onto its back, exposing its belly like a freshly caught fish flopping on the deck of a boat. Never reward the dog for this behavior by giving it a belly rub, no matter how much you want to comfort and reassure it.

The Trouble with Belly Rubs

MANY PEOPLE ENJOY giving a dog a belly rub, and in some cases this is not a problem. But belly rubs often stimulate aggressive behavior in dogs. When young dogs play together and one dog shows another its belly, it expects the other dog to return the favor. The behavior seems to be a form of role playing, in which the dogs practice the meaning of submission and dominance. Thus, if you give a dog a belly rub, the dog will expect to be able to express dominance behavior toward you by putting its paws on you, mouthing you, head butting you, and so on. If you will not tolerate this from the dog, it will try to express dominance toward some other creature, which may well lead to nipping or harassing a child or another vulnerable person.

Characteristics of the Passive Resister

THE PASSIVE RESISTER:

- ❧ Cries and whines and calls out in pain at the slightest provocation.
- ❧ Pees submissively at every turn, runs and hides at the raising of your voice, and comes to you by crawling on its belly. (Of course, the genuinely frightened dog will also display these behaviors. Respond to the truly frightened, or "soft," dog with lots of benevolent eye contact.)
- ❧ Freezes in place when pressured by any request, sometimes even drooling at the mouth for effect.

Unlike the fear biter, who can show some of the same behaviors but never in the same way, the passive resister is as happy as a lark when it gets its own way. It is only when something is asked of the dog that it feels dashed on the rocks of life and becomes a "victim" in the "cruel" hands of its owner.

Training the Passive Resister

NEVER YELL AT or threaten a passive resister. This will only encourage more of the behavior you wish to end. Remember that this dog's behavior is nothing more than a strategy that is natural to all dogs and that you can extinguish it as readily as any other behavior that interferes with training. Be patient and avoid judgments about the dog's state of mind that inhibit your ability to respond appropriately.

The passive resister needs benevolent eye contact more than any other dog. Therefore, you should flood the dog with it, and with treats, pets, and praise for its best efforts. Ignore the dog's "poor, poor, piti-ful me" behavior, and stay neutral unless it complies. And then shower it with reward.

If the passive resister refuses food, which is quite common, put the dog in its crate and try again later. It may help to withhold food at meal-times and only feed the dog for its efforts during training.

Every time the dog flops onto its back or side, walk away with a disdainful attitude. As soon as the dog gets up and follows you, praise it in an upbeat, encouraging tone. When it shivers and shakes on the bench during bench training—again, this is very common with the passive resister—keep it there until it stops shivering no matter how long it takes.

Just as the dominant dog may fight the Halti for hours at a time, the passive resister may shiver and shake on the bench for hours. You must ignore the dog until it lets down and relaxes. As soon as the dog relaxes on the bench, reward it lavishly with lots of treats, pets and praise. Then free the dog from the bench, praise it calmly, and put it in its crate or kennel. Follow the same procedure each day until the dog is happy to climb on the bench and never shivers and shakes on it.

During this period, which may take weeks, you can devote extra five-minute training sessions to clicking and treating for the sit, stand, and down on the ground. After the dog has realized that shivering and shaking on the bench no longer succeed in getting it anywhere and has abandoned the behavior, you can continue with bench training as described in Chapters 10 and 11.

Using the long lines, you should covertly control and interfere with the passive resister's movements as much as or more than with any other dog. Never comfort this dog when it shows distress, unless some accident has occurred and the dog has really been hurt. Never speak to or address the dog while it is resisting in any way, particularly when it shows fearful responses. The dog will do this constantly, no matter how careful you are in handling it. Although in fact you are treating the dog's special needs through training, you must not show the dog that you feel sorry for it or empathize with it. Your mood and attitude toward the dog must remain neutral, becoming positive only when the dog has succeeded in giving the behavior you want.

Like the dominant dog and the active resister, the dog that is a passive resister will eventually come around and become a good and trusted companion.

The Fear Biter
(the Sharp-Shy Dog)

THE FEAR BITER, more accurately called the sharp-shy dog, is every owner's worst nightmare. It owes its temperament to poor breeding and improper socialization. In Europe, breeding regulations ensure that the potentially sharp-shy dog is culled from the litter.

The sharp-shy dog lives in a state of fear brought on by genetics and bad handling. It has exhausted avoidance and submission as defenses, has no escape into compliance, and is left with only the worst kind of aggression to protect itself.

The world this dog inhabits is full of threats, most of them imagined, with which it cannot cope. There is no peace or safety for the dog, or anyone around it. The sharp-shy dog cannot ever be domesticated but always remains essentially savage. It may love you and your family, but it is a threat to every other person that comes within biting distance.

Characteristics of the Fear-Biting, Sharp-Shy Dog

AS A PUPPY the fear-biting, sharp-shy dog:

- ❧ Hides at the back of the breeder's kennel or the animal shelter, shivering with fear.
- ❧ Runs from strangers and new sights and sounds.
- ❧ Barks and bares its teeth, often with raised hackles.
- ❧ Urinates submissively.

In adulthood the sharp-shy dog may often show the same timidity, tugging at your heartstrings and eliciting pity. But because it is overloaded with fear, it can fly unpredictably into violent rages. In these situations, the dog has so exhausted its ability to handle stress that it flees forward. At the shelter, you may see it hurling itself at the kennel wire, mad with aggression.

It is there because other good-hearted people have tried to help it and have failed. It has bitten their children, their friends, and their neighbors. It has ruined their lives and broken their hearts. Even good trainers will fail with this dog, and you should resist the impulse to rescue it.

If the sharp-shy dog is a borderline case, there may be a slim chance for it. But only an expert can assess this with any accuracy. Benevolent eye contact is the best therapy for such a dog, because it lowers the defense responses that drive its problematical behavior.

The bottom line is that it is best to avoid the sharp-shy dog altogether, especially if you have children. No dog is worth risking harm to a child.

17

Behavioral Problems
and How to Solve Them

Everyone wants a quick fix to problems that have taken months or even years to create. A therapist friend of mine once told me that it takes two years to quit smoking and be truly free of the habit. I think his understanding is a little more realistic.

There are two basic ways to deal with canine behavioral problems. The better and more correct method is to retrain the dog and give it a completely new set of behaviors with which to succeed in the world. The more expedient and more often chosen route is to respond to problems in isolation with what are often called "aversives" or "negative reinforcers." Animal behavioral scientists necessarily draw distinctions between these terms and their precise application to different situations that dogs may encounter in the wild or in the human environment. For practical purposes, we are talking about some kind of negative experience that the dog will associate with an unwanted behavior.

If you train a young dog with the system in this book, behavioral problems will likely never occur in the first place, or they will occur in a minimal form that you can manage with a simple "ah–ah!" admonishment and benevolent eye contact. If you are retraining an older dog, my system will give the dog a new picture of the world in which its old behaviors no longer succeed, and the dog will not revert to them.

However, sometimes an older dog is so habituated to a problematical behavior (such as incessant chewing on furniture) that it is helpful to stop the behavior directly so that the dog can progress through training successfully. In all such cases, the following things are necessary if the dog is to have a productive learning experience:

- ❧ The negative stimulus must seem to come from the environment, not from you.
- ❧ The negative stimulus must end at the instant the dog stops the unwanted behavior. As I have said before, the dog must always have an escape from negative experiences in training. In the context of training for obedience, this means teaching the dog a behavior so that it has an understanding of how to do it, before you introduce the compulsion that builds reliability in all circumstances. In the context of using negative reinforcers to solve specific behavioral problems, this means shaping the situation so that the dog's understanding, or its instinctive responses, will help provide it with an immediate way to escape any psychological or physical discomfort.
- ❧ The dog must immediately be rewarded for all positive behaviors.

If the negative reinforcement appears to come from you rather than from the behavior you want stopped, the dog will develop an aversion to you and not the behavior. And then it will wait until you are not present and engage in the unwanted behavior anyway. You must hide the negative reinforcer until the moment it is needed, and never let the dog see that you are responsible for it.

If the negative reinforcement does not stop at the instant the dog stops the unwanted behavior, the dog will be hopelessly confused. If the dog is not immediately rewarded for positive behavior, a wonderful opportunity to confirm a desirable association in the dog's mind has been missed.

How Covert Negative Reinforcers Are Used in Training

A GOOD EXAMPLE of the proper use of covert negative reinforcers is the training of hunting dogs in areas where poisonous snakes are found. Electronic collars are the perfect tool for this job. They allow the trainer to stop a behavior from a distance so that the source of discomfort is undetectable to the dog.

First, a snake is found—trainers in these areas often keep snakes for just this purpose—and the dog is allowed to approach and investigate. Once the dog focuses on the snake, it is "nipped" with the electronic collar so that it associates discomfort with approaching snakes. This is repeated as often as necessary, but once is usually enough to teach the dog to stay as far away from snakes as possible. Far better the dog feel a moment's discomfort and concern than die a slow, painful death from snakebite.

This work is usually best done with the help of a professional trainer who understands both the proper use of the tools and the safety requirements for the dog. But observe here how the dog's instincts are recruited on its own behalf and how the dog has the option to reapproach the snake or not.

Rummaging in the Garbage

THE SAME BASIC idea lies behind the strategy of putting something on the lid of a garbage can that will make a startling noise if the dog disturbs it. It could be a mousetrap that will pop up in the air and snap shut, a balloon taped to the lid that the dog will burst, or a personal security "screamer." (In case you are wondering, I have never heard of a mousetrap snapping shut on a dog's nose or paw. Dogs are too quick for that to be a problem.)

The success of this covert negative reinforcer depends on the dog's individual sensitivity to noise. Some dogs may be cured of trying to get the lid off the garbage can after one explosion of noise, some may need several such experiences, and others may not be bothered by any number of them. If your dog is rummaging in the garbage and you want to experiment with this method, try it every day for a week to see if it will succeed.

I prefer to put garbage totally out of reach of the dog, however, by placing the container in a cabinet under the sink or somewhere else inaccessible. Why invite the problem in the first place?

Jumping Up

JUMPING UP IS another frequent complaint, and many dog training books advise readers to "knee the dog in the chest" or "step on the dog's toes," and so forth, usually as part of the general strategy of being the dog's alpha pack leader. The theory is that the alpha dog quickly and roughly disciplines any dog that has the temerity to jump up on it, and so should you.

Such "solutions" only make the dog connect the unpleasant experience of being kneed or stepped on with you rather than with jumping up on you. As a result, the dog becomes reluctant to recall close to you, or to recall at all. Or it accepts your dominance and jumps on other people, usually the kids; just as in the wild pack, the dog that has been prevented from jumping up on the alpha dog will then jump up on a weaker member of the pack. Or it does all these things at different times.

This is an example of how behavior and consequence must be directly linked in dog training. If there is a break in the chain, there is no way for the dog to form the desired association between its behavior and the consequence. Alpha pack leader responses to jumping up cause the dog to form an association between you and the negative reinforcer, which stops all further learning instead of stopping the unwanted behavior.

You can cure dogs of jumping up on you in a few minutes by doing nothing more than stepping out of the way when they attempt to put their feet on you and then reinforcing the sit, stand, or down with the clicker and food treats when the dog misses you and eventually tries something else. Remember that dogs only repeat behaviors that succeed and quickly abandon behaviors that fail. You can now pass the clicker and treats to any youngster or other person who may be vulnerable to the jumping up, and they can teach the dog the same lesson without risking a fight or being violent.

Paws and Praise

FOR DOGS THAT are severely habituated to jumping up or have status problems, there is a more direct method that I call "paws and praise."

Begin by calling your dog to you and encouraging it to jump up on you. When the dog does jump up, praise it heartily and look it in the face while you search with your hands for its paws.

Once you find the dog's paws, begin to squeeze them gently. Slowly increase the pressure on them while you praise more and more enthusiastically.

As the dog begins to show that its paws are becoming uncomfortable, lower them to the ground, praising all the while.

The instant the dog's front paws touch the ground, release them, but continue to praise and pet for at least thirty seconds and perhaps even introduce some treats.

After a few minutes, repeat the exercise by encouraging the dog to jump up once again. Two or three of these exercises a day over a week and the dog will never jump up again.

Empowering the Dog to Solve Its Own Behavior Problems—Part 1

LET'S LOOK CLOSELY at why the dog jumps up and how different responses on your part give the dog different ideas about "what happens next," evoke different moods in the dog during training, and produce dramatically different results. Your dog jumps up on you to demand your attention. This behavior has overtones of dominance. The dog may be expressing joy to see you, which is why so many people tolerate, and thus tacitly encourage, this behavior. But that joy is shaped by the dog's feelings of insecurity in its status relative to you.

If your response is to knock the dog down or step on its toes, you are "fighting" with, or dominating, it. That means you are inviting more jumping up from any dominant dog. And you are frightening any submissive dog (even submissive dogs are expressing conflict about their status when they jump up), with the risk that the dog may become fearful of you. Not to mention that you have put yourself on the same footing as the dog, for you have made yourself a dog by engaging in a canine behavior. In doing so, you have forced your dog to respond to you, according to its temperament, as it would to an alpha dog.

That is not how I want my dog to respond to me. If my dog's status is dominant, I don't want to alter its status. But I also don't want to have to reassert my dominance over it constantly as if I were a pack member. I want the dog to see me as a partner, not a competitor. If my dog is submissive, I don't want it to shrink from me. I want to build up its confidence.

Seasoned parents and other caregivers will recognize that acting like a dominant alpha pack leader to your dog is like fighting with a young child. You might decide that it is worthwhile to argue with a teenager, but fighting with children just makes you into another child in their eyes, a child who can be challenged over and over again. Likewise, the dog that you have dominated will continue to test the situation in an attempt to dominate you. Or if it can't dominate you, it will find weaker human beings to test.

The paws-and-praise technique does not seek to dominate the dog. It enlists the dog's decision making on its own behalf. When you invite the dog to jump up on you, there is no fight and you appear friendly and positive. When you praise the dog for jumping up, it believes you are happy with its behavior.

Then the dog's front paws begin to be uncomfortable as you hold them with gradually increasing pressure. Because your mood and affect toward the dog are positive and cheerful, the dog cannot identify its discomfort as coming from you.

When you lower the dog to the ground and all four feet are down, the discomfort ceases. Because you continue to praise and act happy, the dog believes the discomfort must have come from the act of jumping up, not from you. The dog got attention and pets whether it was up on you or had all four feet on the ground.

It doesn't take much of this for the dog to decide that jumping up is a losing proposition. Dogs that decide for themselves to cease a behavior never repeat it. On the other hand, the old adage "a man convinced against his will is of the same opinion still" applies as well to dogs as it does to people.

If you use a negative reinforcer, you can see how important it is to hide the fact that it comes from you. Again, if the dog sees you as a link in the chain, it will only stop the unwanted behavior in your presence. For there to be a reliable change, the dog must decide to stop the behavior for its own reasons.

THERE IS ONE more thing to consider in relation to a dog's jumping up on you. Even when it is stimulated by anxiety in the dog about its status relative to you, the behavior also has a positive aspect in training for some types of work. The dog is willingly committing its body to yours. From the standpoint of effective training, this is not a behavior we should try to stamp out because doing so can undermine our bond with the dog. Instead, we should try to channel and adapt the behavior in order to create a stronger bond with the dog and heighten its ability to cooperate with our wishes.

The best way to deal with the dog's jumping up on others, especially children, is through the use of the long lines in the course of informal training as described in Chapter 5. This will teach the dog that it must not jump up on other people. Training the obedience behaviors as described in Part III of this book will help manage the dog's eagerness to jump up on you and keep it from getting out of control. Then you can still have the benefit of the dog's willingness to put its body in contact with yours, which is a crucial sign that the dog feels a strong, positive bond with you.

If the dog's jumping up is uncontrollable by other means, then the paws-and-praise method will work. But before you apply a solution to a problem, it is important to consider that it may have undesirable consequences as well. This is why it is much more effective to deal with behavioral issues through an integrated training, or retraining, process, rather than by trying to solve specific problems in isolation.

Pulling on the Leash

ANOTHER FREQUENT COMPLAINT is that the dog pulls on the leash while walking. Like jumping up and all other canine behavior problems, pulling on the leash is best solved by using a proper training system. However, sometimes a more direct method, employing a subtle covert negative reinforcer, is useful.

To deal directly with leash problems, you will need a special tool called the Halti head collar. Invented by Dr. Roger Mugford, an English veterinarian, the Halti head collar has done more than perhaps any other

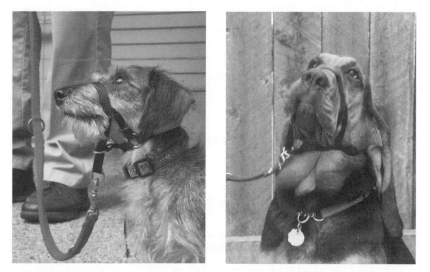

Haltis are for dogs of all sizes and dispositions. Here is the Halti properly fitted. Notice the loose leash.

product to improve the lives of dogs. Unfortunately, it is often mistakenly ignored in favor of other collars and leaders that also claim to prevent pulling on the leash but do not. The Halti is one product for which there truly is no substitute.

The Halti is a head harness much like those used on horses. Its value over other methods and tools used to prevent pulling is immeasurable. It inflicts no pain whatsoever, moderates the dog's status, and takes almost no strength to use correctly. Here is how to do it:

- ❧ At the dog's daily walk time, put the Halti on and adjust the head strap so that it fits snugly. Tightening the strap is important because the dog may reach up with its paws and try to swipe the Halti off, or it may try to rub the Halti off on an object or the ground. If the dog manages to remove the Halti during the first few tries, it will likely continue trying to remove it whenever you put it on.
- ❧ Attach your leash to the ring that hangs below the dog's muzzle. The ring is sewn to a cinching device that closes the dog's mouth when the dog pulls against it. Although there is no physical pain, dogs detest having their mouths shut against their will. This gentle cinching device separates the Halti from all other head collars and leaders.
- ❧ Holding the leash, praise the dog and throw treats to it.

Make your dog's first experience wearing a Halti a positive one: keep things happy and upbeat, and make sure your dog sees lots of reward.

Your dog may need a little time to adjust to the Halti.

❧ Keep the dog on a loose leash while you move about casually in one area. If the dog fights the Halti by swiping at it or trying to rub it off, pull up on the leash until the dog's snout is pointed upward and it cannot hook its paw on the leash. This prevents the dog from using the leash as leverage in an effort to pull the Halti off.

At first, your dog may try to remove the Halti. To correct this behavior, look away and show a neutral body posture, pulling gently on the leash so that your dog's nose points to the sky.

- Avoid speaking to the dog while doing the previous step. It is also a good idea to turn your head away and only look at the dog with your peripheral vision. Most important, do not scold the dog for fighting the Halti. This only encourages the dog to connect you with its mouth being shut.
- The instant the dog stops fighting the Halti, let the leash go loose so that the dog can drop its head and open its mouth. Now abandon your neutrality and become totally involved in the dog's well-being by praising it effusively and giving it treats.

When your dog accepts the Halti, heap on rewards and affection!

- Repeat this exercise until the dog begins to understand that fighting the Halti brings discomfort and that accepting it produces treats, praise, and positive attention from you.

❧ This procedure can take anything from one to several days to complete. Make your sessions a few minutes long at first, and increase the time as you go along.

❧ The leash must either be completely slack when the dog is cooperating or completely tight, holding the dog's nose in the air, whenever it is fighting the Halti. The mistake most people make with the Halti is to allow there to be tension on the leash while the Halti is in use.

❧ Used correctly, the Halti separates you from any association the dog might form in struggling against it. For that reason, it is very important that you remain quiet and calm while this struggle is going on between the dog and its perceived environment. You want to remain neutral and indifferent to the dog's behavior and offer no clue as to the preferred outcome.

❧ Do not take the dog for a walk after you have removed the Halti. You may play fetch in the yard or do a click-and-treat session on sits, stands, and downs if you like. But from this point on the dog must walk on the Halti until its lesson is learned.

❧ When the dog begins to abandon the idea of fighting the Halti, you may begin to walk it about. Your job is to keep the leash loose at all times.

❧ At first you should walk in a completely unpredictable way, changing direction and speed constantly as you go along. But do so without ever jerking hard on the leash as you would with a choke chain or pinch collar. You may try at this point to make benevolent eye contact and drop treats from your mouth during the walk.

❧ You will notice the dog beginning to watch you more and more carefully. Praise and reward this!

❧ Over a few weeks the dog will accept that the Halti is part of its opportunity to get out and about. When the dog's behavior improves, begin your walk with the Halti on and then remove it partway through the walk and put it in your pocket. If the dog starts to pull on the leash attached to the flat collar, calmly put the Halti back on and continue as if nothing has changed.

❧ When the dog's behavior on the leash becomes more consistent, you can begin the walk with the Halti in your pocket and use it only as needed. The Halti is a tool; it should not be a permanent fixture on the dog. You use it to teach and then remove it to "proof" the dog's behavior. The dog will soon decide that walking quietly with the leash attached to the flat collar is much nicer than wearing the Halti, and then you can put the Halti away permanently.

So far, so good. But just as measures to stop a dog from jumping up on you or other people may have an undesirable side effect, so can use of the Halti in some cases. By the very nature of training, our interactions with the dog produce undesirable as well as desirable effects, and we must take all these effects into account.

The Halti moderates a dog's drive and lowers its status, and this can produce depression. Likewise, if the dog strenuously and persistently resists the Halti, its attitude toward walking at the heel may be negatively affected. This negativity toward walking at the heel may also take on overtones of defense: The dog sees the Halti as an attack and perceives its resistance as an act of self-protection from the handler. This is certainly not the kind of mood we want to create in the dog.

Remember that as we discussed in Chapter 4, the mood that a dog associates with a behavior will affect the reliability of that behavior. This is not to mention that the dog has a reasonable right to enjoy its walks. We must therefore pay careful attention to the dog's mood and do any additional training needed to make it happy on our walks together.

If we see that the dog is becoming depressed and/or negatively disposed to the heel after we introduce the Halti, we must remediate the dog's mood and help it form a positive association with the Halti. The answer is to find a behavior that will trigger a positive mood in the dog that we can attach to the Halti by association. As the down can be used to change the dog's mood and reduce aggression to other dogs (see "Manipulating Mood in Training" in Chapter 4), the game of fetch can make the dog feel more positive about the heel and the Halti.

As I explained in describing how to teach a dog to play fetch in Chapter 5, this game satisfies a dog's prey drive. By its nature, prey drive contains little or no defense response and therefore always creates a positive mood. The only problem in its use is controlling the amount of prey drive we raise in the dog so that it can maintain control of its own emotions. If we build the prey drive up too much, the dog can become what is known as "ball crazy" and tune out training.

If you watch sports on television, you have probably seen highlights of athletes running headlong into things, referees, spectators, or television crews in what commentators often call blind pursuit of the ball.

The athlete in question consciously sees nothing besides the ball and has even forgotten about his or her own safety. This is a human example of prey drive at its most powerful. In this state of mind the rest of the world, including even the slightest hint of fear and anxiety, disappears and there is only the joy of the chase. Mood cannot be more perfectly attuned to behavior than this, and there is no better tool to use to remedy any self-concern created in the dog during training.

If you have not already taught your dog to play fetch as described in Chapter 5, do so now. And then take your dog into a suitable training area, such as a large backyard or an open field. You should, of course, only engage the dog's prey drive in safe surroundings and situations, where the dog cannot run into traffic or other problems. Put the dog on a long line to ensure that you maintain control of the game, and:

- Bring out the Kong, my preferred fetch toy, or another suitable fetch object (never a tennis ball; see Chapter 5).
- Show the dog the Kong to engage its prey drive, and briefly hide the Kong behind your back in order to raise drive further and excite the dog (do not tease the dog by holding the Kong behind your back for more than a second or two, but instead throw it as soon as the dog becomes excited).
- Throw the Kong a short distance, perhaps fifteen to twenty feet. If you throw the Kong too far, the dog may use up its energy in running and have none left for learning something new. Short throws also mean less trouble getting the Kong back from the dog, because you can use the long line to do so if the dog is reluctant to return to you with its prize. Don't worry about training the retrieve now; that is something you can work on separately in other games of fetch, if necessary. What you are working on here is mood.
- Do not tug or yank on the Kong when you are taking it from the dog. If the dog does not want to release the Kong, hook a finger or two of one hand under the dog's flat collar and only let the dog feel pressure on the collar while you wiggle the Kong out of the dog's mouth with your other hand. Show the dog a cheerful, playful mood as you do this, the opposite of a stern, determined tug of war.
- Give the dog a few more short throws of the Kong until it is happily committed to the game, and then begin to hold the Kong under your chin with your hand and start walking slowly

in a straight line. The dog's focus on the Kong will let you move around so as to maneuver the dog into the heel position at your left side.

☙ The instant the dog arrives in this position, throw the Kong a short distance away, within the length of the long line. Again, short throws save the dog's energy for learning the point of this exercise and make it easier for you to get the Kong back.

☙ Playfully get the Kong back and repeat this behavior until the dog starts assuming the heel position on its own in an attempt to "force" the throw from you. When this happens, try taking a step or two forward before throwing.

☙ Say "yes" as you step forward to trigger benevolent eye contact and thus help begin moving the dog's attention in walking beside from you from the Kong to your eyes, which is what you will want at the completion of training the heel. At this point you can also try removing your hand from the Kong and simply holding it tucked under your chin to heighten the dog's focus on the Kong and your face.

Expect to do this for several sessions over the course of a week or so. I think you will find it a fun exercise that you will want to do, and I know the dog will enjoy the chance to satisfy its instinctive desire to chase.

When the dog is comfortable walking beside you for five steps or more, you can introduce the Halti back onto the dog and continue the game as before. Do not hook the Halti up to your leash at first, however, so that the dog has no negative association with the Halti beyond the fact of wearing it. For covert control, attach the long line to the dog's flat collar.

Watch to be sure the dog's mood does not fall back into depression or unhappiness. Your enthusiasm for the game and praise and encouragement will help a lot here! If the dog is not ready for the Halti yet, you will see this in its demeanor. Just play the game without the Halti for a few more sessions and try again. When the dog is tolerating the Halti well, proceed as follows:

☙ Attach the long line to the dog's flat collar, but do not attach the leash to the Halti yet.

☙ Alternate walking a few paces in the heel position, keeping the

Kong tucked under your chin, with short throws of the Kong for the dog to fetch, or dropping the Kong to the dog directly from under your chin by lifting your head.

❧ When the dog is comfortable with this, begin to play the game with the leash attached to the Halti and the long line still attached to the flat collar.

❧ Again alternate walking a few paces in the heel position, keeping the Kong tucked under your chin, with short throws of the Kong for the dog to fetch, dropping the leash when you throw. This allows the dog to chase the Kong, dragging the leash behind it.

❧ Use the long line to interrupt the dog if it tries to get the Halti off or to ensure that you can get the Kong back.

Over time you can increase the number of steps you take while the dog is in the heel position until it will follow you all over the place in expectation of a throw of the Kong. Be careful not to hold the Kong so long that the dog loses enthusiasm or loses faith that you will throw it.

This exercise will wipe away any negative mood associated with the Halti and replace it with a happy one. The process takes a little time, but if you are patient and consistent, it will produce a much more cheerful, confident dog and greatly benefit the rest of its training.

Until pulling on the leash is fully resolved, including any negative reactions to the Halti, you must therefore treat all walks as training walks. People often become frustrated because they want to combine their own exercise walking or running with the dog's outings at too early a stage. Be patient in helping the dog learn to walk comfortably alongside you and you will then be able to enjoy years of comfortable walks or jogs together.

Empowering the Dog to
Solve Its Own Behavior Problems—Part 2

LET'S LOOK AT the psychological picture you have now painted for your dog with the Halti. Constantly praising and rewarding the dog when its focus comes off the Halti makes it see you in a very positive light. It does not appear that you are causing its discomfort when it fights the Halti, and in fact you are not.

The dog decides whether it will have its mouth closed by the Halti or be able to open and close its mouth at will. The dog is the master of its own destiny. If the dog pulls on the leash or fights the Halti, it experiences the frustration of being unable to open its mouth. If it does not pull on the leash or fight the Halti, it has full freedom to open and close its mouth. Dogs are very mouth-focused animals and they hate not to have full control of their mouths. This is a powerful motivation for the dog to accept the Halti and stop pulling on the leash.

If you do not draw any attention to yourself when the Halti is keeping the dog's mouth closed, the dog will not see you as part of its predicament. Thus, whenever the dog fights the leash, you adopt a neutral, silent pose. You never scold the dog or give it an opportunity to associate your behavior with its experience, even though you are the one lifting up on the leash. As long as the dog does not pull, it is free to do what it wants. Just as with the paws-and-praise method, the dog cannot detect your involvement because your behavior offers no clue to that fact. If the Halti should cause any problems of its own, you can remediate them straightforwardly with behaviors, such as highly rewarding games of fetch with the Halti on, that give the dog a positive association with it.

Now contrast the autonomy and dignity that these techniques give the dog with the use of classical conditioning with a choke chain or pinch collar. When you jerk on a choke chain or pinch collar, the dog has no way to escape the discomfort. There is also no question in the dog's mind that you are responsible for its discomfort. With proper use of the Halti, as with my training system as a whole, the dog always has an escape. It always has a choice that will allow it to avoid even the slightest hint of discomfort and to win reward, praise, and affection.

Aggression to Other Dogs

AGGRESSION TO OTHER dogs is a complex problem with no simple, expedient solution. Before following the steps below, you may find it helpful to review "Manipulating Mood in Training" in Chapter 4, which explores the problem and how to solve it from a conceptual point of view.

In a nutshell, the idea is to put the dog into a behavior that will alter its mood from an anxious, fearful, and aggressive state of mind to a calm and contented one. The default control behavior, the down, is the best behavior for this (for training a happy, confident down, see Chapters 8 and 9). If you have created a good positive down in the dog:

- ❧ Signal for the down on the first sign of aggression toward another dog.
- ❧ Keep the dog in the down until it relaxes into the position and waits for you to release it with the word "free."
- ❧ When you see your dog relax into a calmer mood, immediately signal "free." When you free the dog, get its attention by saying "yes" to trigger benevolent eye contact (see Chapter 7), and reward it heavily for focusing on you.
- ❧ If it is too hard for your dog to stay down because the other dog keeps coming closer, as may often happen in a public park, work on this problem in a situation where the other dog is handled by a friend or is behind a fence.

If you put your dog in a down whenever it shows aggression toward another dog, the sight of another dog will gradually begin to trigger a calm mood, rather than an anxious, fearful, and therefore aggressive one. As I mentioned in Chapter 4, this process will take time. But if you are patient and consistent in your approach, you will create a permanent change in the dog and you will never have to deal with dog aggression again.

Aggression at the Door

AGGRESSION AT THE door is similarly complex, and it has a similar solution. The dog is aggressive when visitors or delivery people arrive at the door because it is anxious about your reaction to these events. The dog's anxious mood then drives anxious behavior that may include barking furiously at visitors or trying to nip or bite them.

The solution is to put the dog into a behavior that will alter its mood. For more on mood and its meaning in training, see Chapter 4. As mentioned in that chapter, the best behavior for altering mood is the down. If you have created a good, positive down in the dog, you should immediately signal for it on the first sign of aggression at the door.

If you do not have a good down, keep the dog safe and comfortable in its crate when you expect visitors, and put the dog in the crate when you must answer the door unexpectedly. Until you have trained a happy, confident, relaxed down, attempts to handle aggression at the door in other ways will only make the situation worse.

After you have trained a good down, proceed as follows:

- ❧ Schedule a visit by a friend. Arrange with the friend that he or she will knock or ring the bell only once, and then be prepared to wait until you open the door.
- ❧ At the appointed time, have the dog at your side with the long line attached to the flat collar, and await your friend's ring or knock at a distance away from the door that is greater than the length of the line.
- ❧ If the dog charges the door at the sound of the doorbell or knock, stand on the line with your back turned to the dog. Keep your back turned for a moment after the dog comes to the end of the line and knocks itself down with the force of its own momentum, to allow the dog time to get back on its feet and see that you and your hands are not responsible for what happened.
- ❧ Turn around, call the dog to you, and reassure it with benevolent eye contact, a treat, and a pet.
- ❧ If the dog does not charge the door at the sound of the knock or the ringing of the bell, it will almost certainly still be feeling some agitation and concern, so reassure it with benevolent eye contact, a treat, and a pet. By the way, if this is how the dog reacts, it is a great sign that training is going well, so give yourself a big pat on the back.
- ❧ Walk to the door with the dog and put it in a down.
- ❧ Open the door and welcome the visitor into the house while the dog remains in the down. This gives the dog an opportunity to see and sniff the visitor from a little distance and to observe that the two of you are interacting comfortably.
- ❧ Continue to stand talking quietly with the visitor until you see the dog relax into the down and any remaining tension go out of its body. During this time you can give the visitor a biscuit or other treat for the dog.
- ❧ Say "free" and let the dog come up to sniff the visitor more closely. The visitor should look away from the dog and hold the treat out in the palm of his or her hand for the dog to take.

- Once the dog has taken the treat, calmly walk the visitor to wherever in the house you are going to spend a little time.
- For the next few days, repeat the procedure with different friends, neighbors, or relatives the dog has not met.
- For the next few weeks, put the dog in a down every time someone comes to the door.

Putting the dog in the down when someone comes to the door initiates a two-stage process over time. First, a visitor's arrival will become a signal for your dog to down. The down will provide the dog with an escape from its anxiety because you will never let your dog up until its mood has changed.

Gradually the arrival of visitors will become the signal for your dog to change to a relaxed mood or for an already relaxed mood to strengthen. A dog in a happy, relaxed mood is unlikely to be aggressive, and your problem is solved. This process will take time, and you need to be patient. The change in your dog will be permanent, however, and you will never have to deal with aggression at the door again.

Mouthing and Nipping

A dog should never be allowed to mouth and nip people or "communicate" with them in this way as it does with other dogs. To let this go unchecked may lead to the dog biting someone seriously. Complicating matters further is that this problem must be solved when the dog is a young puppy. If a dog six months or older exhibits this behavior, you need the help of an expert trainer.

The usual ways that people are advised to stop a dog from mouthing and nipping, such as clamping the dog's mouth shut or rapping it on the mouth, may seem to work in the moment. But in fact they only worsen the problem and increase the likelihood that the dog will injure a person by biting.

To stop puppies from mouthing and nipping:

- Get down on the floor with the puppy and wiggle your hand in front of its mouth to invite a nip. What you are doing here is mimicking the behavior of prey animals, as children unwittingly do before they are nipped.

❧ As soon as the puppy's mouth touches your hand, scream as if you are in agony, jump away from the puppy, and turn your back to it. I like to go and face the wall with my head bowed. The point of this behavior is to show the puppy that unlike its thick-skinned littermates, you are too sensitive to endure any contact from its mouth.

❧ Repeat this procedure several times a day, if the puppy will even mouth you at all after this experience.

Very few puppies will continue to mouth and nip after you do this once, much less two or three times. If a puppy does persist in mouthing and nipping:

❧ Lay the back of your stronger hand against the puppy's head, and wiggle the other hand in front of its mouth.

❧ When the puppy's mouth touches your wiggling hand, shout "No!" in a commanding voice, and with the back of your other hand, push the puppy away forcefully. What you are doing here is imitating the behavior of a female dog with her puppies when one of them suckles too hard.

No puppy should continue to mouth and nip after this happens to it once or twice. And it will observe this prohibition with all people, not just with you.

Begging at the Table

IF YOU FEED or put the dog in its crate at the same time that you eat your meals, there will be no problem with it begging for food at the table. If you want the dog to be loose around mealtime, however, you can take the following steps:

❧ Put the dog on a tie-out at the dinner table. A leash looped around a table leg will do nicely.

❧ Have everyone at the table ignore the dog completely—and, of course, give it no food—while they eat.

❧ Keep the dog on the tie-out until everyone is finished eating and the table has been cleared.

❧ Then free the dog and give it a pet and a treat or its own meal.

At first the dog will respond by whining for food and attention while you eat. But if you steadfastly ignore it, the dog will eventually relax and even go to sleep. This is another case (see the techniques in the preceding section for solving aggression toward other dogs or toward visitors at the door) where without hurting the dog in any way you put it in a position where it cannot do wrong and you do not allow it to move until its mood changes. Eventually your sitting down to eat will be a physiological signal for the dog to fall asleep.

Making Sure Baby and Dog Get Along

A COMMON AND difficult problem for families is the introduction of a baby into a household with a dog. This should be handled in a similar way to the introduction of a second dog, as described in Chapter 15.

Even before the baby leaves the hospital, you can bring home one of the baby's blankets or an article of its clothing for the dog to sniff and become accustomed to the baby's scent. Give the dog some pets and a treat when you do this to begin building a strong positive association to the baby in the dog's mind.

The first meeting of dog and baby should happen outside the house on the front lawn or sidewalk. Let the dog sniff, nuzzle, and lick the baby. Then reward the dog hugely at this moment, again to build a strong positive association to the baby in the dog's mind.

From that point on, tie the appearance of the child to huge rewards for the dog. For example, when the baby wakes and is brought out for feeding, the dog should be given lots of treats and attention. When the baby goes back to bed, the treats and attention should disappear. The contrast between the two situations will accelerate the process of building a bond between baby and dog. The dog will begin to desire the baby's presence, because it is getting its best rewards at the same time that the baby is receiving attention.

The common mistake that people make is to shower the baby with attention and affection in front of the dog while giving the dog no attention and affection. This produces resentment in the dog about the baby's presence.

Another common mistake is to take privileges away from the dog at the appearance of the baby. For example, the dog is no longer allowed on the bed or sofa or allowed into the nursery—or even the house—after the baby arrives. If you intend to change things in your home for the dog, do this well before the baby arrives so no association is made by the dog between these events. It is best to begin this change in the first trimester so that the dog has plenty of time to accept its new circumstances.

If you make it clear to the dog that the baby is its greatest ally in winning reward and attention, the dog will love and protect the child forever. The dog then sees the baby as the bringer of all that is good, not the end of its status and privileges.

IN REGARD TO all canine behavioral problems, please remember that an ounce of prevention with the right training, or retraining, is worth tons of curative quick fixes.

Conclusion:
A New View of Dogs

More than any specific concept or technique, this book has aimed to give you a new and different view of dogs and how to train them. There is always much to learn each day when working with dogs, whether you are a first-time owner or an experienced trainer, and this process never ends. The system I have presented here is directed toward making both the trainer and the dog open to new possibilities. It seeks to move the dog's mind rather than its body, based on the theory that "where the mind goes, the body will follow." And it also seeks to move the owner into seeing dogs in a new, exciting light. Dogs are wonderful creatures, and their psychology and behavior are complex and fascinating.

This idea presents itself as somewhat counterintuitive to the common understanding of the training of dogs and the supposed necessity to control them with rigid commands. With a little patience and imagination, and the information and methods in this book, you can take the much more productive route of letting the dog decide to cooperate with your wishes of its own free will. This will dramatically improve your relationship with your dog and the quality of your life together. Be firm and fair, remembering that violence begets violence and that time and patience almost always win the day.

In doing so, you will see your dog's mind open and its understanding and confidence grow. You will see the dog's increasing responsiveness to you develop into cooperative obedience that is leash- and handler-independent.

Your relationship with a dog that you have wisely and carefully trained will be richly rewarding in itself, and do wonders for your physical, mental, and emotional health. Not least of its benefits is that it will connect you to nature in a way that has become all too rare in the modern world.

Owning and training a dog should be fun and beneficial to all involved. I hope I have offered you a better way to experience this process.

Resources

Books for General Information

Book of Dogs: A Complete Medical Reference Guide for Dogs and Puppies. Faculty and Staff, School of Veterinary Medicine University of California, Davis. Edited by Mordecai Siegal. New York: HarperCollins, 1995.

The Complete Dog Book. American Kennel Club. 20th Edition. New York: Ballantine Books, 2006.

Dog Owner's Home Veterinary Handbook. James M. Giffin M.D., and Liisa D. Carlson, D.V.M.

Encyclopedia of Dog Breeds. Caroline D.Coile, Ph.D. 2nd ed. Hauppauge, NY: Barron's Educational Series, 2005.

The New Encyclopedia of the Dog. Bruce Fogle. New York: Dorling Kindersley, 2000.

Books for Deeper Understanding

Beyond Freedom and Dignity. B. F. Skinner. 1971. Reprint, Cambridge, MA: Hackett Publishing Company, 2002.

Don't Shoot the Dog: The New Art of Teaching and Training. Karen Pryor. New York: Bantam Doubleday Dell, 1985.

Genetics and the Social Behavior of the Dog. John Paul Scott and John L. Fuller. Chicago: University of Chicago Press, 1998.

The New Knowledge of Dog Behavior, Clarence Pfaffenberger.
Wenatchee, WA: Dogwise Publishing, 2001.
On Aggression. Konrad Lorenz. 1974. Reprint, MJF Books, 1997.
Training Dogs: A Manual. Konrad Most, Wenatchee, WA: Dogwise
Publishing, 2001.

Organizations

American Kennel Club, www.akc.org
Canadian Kennel Club, www.ckc.org
United Schutzhund Clubs of America,
www.germanshepherddog.com
Many other organizations devoted to specific breeds and dog-related
activities can be found on the Internet.

Acknowledgments

If there is anything I have learned in writing this book, it is that it takes more than an author to bring a book to completion. With that in mind, I want to thank the people who have made this book possible.

First I would like to thank my literary agent, David Vigliano. It is no exaggeration to say that without his belief in me and willingness to pursue this project, it would never have existed. To him I extend my eternal gratitude for giving me this opportunity.

A tip of the hat to Kirby Kim, also of Vigliano and Associates, for his many efforts on my behalf.

To Hilary Hinzmann, who shepherded me, with endless patience, through the process of writing my first book, thank you.

To my editors, Renee Sedliar of Avalon Publishing and Brad Wilson of HarperCollins Canada, thank you for taking a chance on a dog trainer and aspiring author from Robert's Creek, B.C., and for guiding and supporting my efforts to create a truly unique and useful book on the training of dogs.

To my photographer, Georgia Combes, who brought to the project not only her camera and her artist's eye but her boundless enthusiasm and love of dogs, thank you.

To my wife, Laurie, and my daughter Rosalee, who shared every step along the way and gave of their time and energy in more ways than can ever be acknowledged, thank you.

No dog trainer learns in a vacuum. All of us who work with dogs are indebted to those who have trained before us and without whose efforts there would be no path to follow.

I owe a great debt of knowledge about dogs to Judge Eileen Fraser, who generously shared her endless wisdom and advice during my "years in the wilderness" looking for a true and complete method of training dogs, and who introduced me to the work of the founding father of all modern dog training, Konrad Most, without whose insights we would still all be lost; Dennis Brunton, who befriended me and taught me about the importance of understanding the owner as well as the dog; the many great trainers of our day, including Gottfried Dildei, Stuart Hilliard, Gary Patterson, and Tom Rose, who were a never-ending source of information and inspiration and who have devoted their lives to the working dog and its well-being and service to people; Karen Pryor, who brought about a revolution in the use of stress-free teaching methods in dog training; B. F. Skinner, whose research gave Pryor the ammunition to start that revolution; and Konrad Lorenz, whose study of aggression is the basis for so much of modern animal behavioral science.

Finally, I want to express my gratitude to the friends who have endlessly supported me on my journey with dogs. Thanks to Eileen Porter for her efforts on my behalf; Gil Cates and Judith Reichman for their friendship, wisdom, and advice; and Peter Alpert, Susan Roth, and Paul and Penny Senov for their many years of friendship and support for my methods.

Index

A

ability to master complex tasks
  hunting and herding, 4–5
  selective breeding and, 5, 43,
    45–47
  state of mind and, 7, 55–56,
    61–62
  See also decision making; winning
    response
accepting dogs "as is"
  adaptability, 4, 11, 88
  observational skills, 5, 55, 85
  overview, xix–xx, 3, 6
  See also ability to master complex
    tasks; difficult dogs; instinc-
    tual drives
active resister dogs, 118, 181, 188–90
adaptability, 4, 11, 88
aggression
  as defensive response, 11, 13
  fear-driven, 103
  as fight prevention, 99
  to other dogs, 60–61, 210–11
  possessiveness, 87–88, 180,
    183–84
  as protective response, 182–83

responding to, with overwhelming force, 186
time out in crate for, 185
to visitors, 211–13
See also bites and biting
aggressive dogs
  avoiding operant conditioning,
    30, 36, 117
  Jack Russell Terriers, 40
  teaching release to, 87
  See also dominant dogs
ah–ah admonition, 84, 134,
  144–45, 157, 178
alpha dominance of dogs, 3, 14–15,
  102
alpha dominance of trainer, 14–15,
  183, 198. *See also* classical
  conditioning
American Kennel Club (AKC),
  40–41, 43
association, learning by, 57–59,
  159. *See also* negative associations; positive associations
aversives. *See* negative reinforcers
avoidance as defensive response,
  11–13, 32, 131

signals for, 84–85
instinctual drives
    creating unpleasantness for, 26
    defense responses, 11–13, 32,
        131, 171
    dominance and, 182
    frustration and, 60, 94
    perpetuate successful behaviors,
        5, 7
    prey drive, 39–40, 87, 206–7
    utilization of, 10, 207–9
    to win access to resources, 4
    See also aggression; rewards; sub-
        mission; winning response
intermediate training, 147–58
    bench training for clarifying win-
        ning response, 152–53, 158
    building reliability, 150–52
    overview, 147–48
    stay, 156–58
    strengthening contact, 148–50
    working without a leash, 154–58

J

Jack Russell Terriers, 40
jealousy between dogs, avoiding,
    179–80
jumping up, dealing with, 197–201

K

kennels, 70, 91, 101. *See also* crate
    training
Kong, 207–9

L

learning and discovery
    as goal of training, xxi
    safe place is next to trainer,
        79–82, 95
    self-achieved, 119
    See also stress, learning without
leash, working without, 154–58
leash training, 94–96, 186–87,
    201–9
lines of different lengths, 22–25,
    74–75, 86. *See also* long lines

littermates, 175
long lines
    with active resisters, 190
    in dog park, 100
    for jumping up prevention,
        200–201
    with passive resisters, 192
    tightrope walking down, 155,
        158, 164
    training method, 76–82
    for training recall behavior,
        162–64
    for working without a leash,
        154–55, 158
    See also covert control

M

manipulating moods, 60–61
moods of dogs
    dance of joy and, 65–66,
        150–52, 153, 158, 171
    happy and confident, visualizing,
        62–65, 108–9
    manipulating, 60–61, 211–13
    optimal, for training, 61–62
    overview, 56–60
    remediating, 206–9
    visualizing your dog's, 62–65,
        108–9
moods of trainer. *See* patience;
    trainer's demeanor
mouth, hiding treats in the,
    114–15, 148–49, 162, 164
mouthing and nipping, 213–14
Mugford, Roger, 201
multiple dogs, 175–80

N

name of dog
    association with pain, 8, 18
    attaching positive association to,
        85
    using for recall, 162
naming behaviors, 26, 118, 123–26
negative associations
    dog's name and pain, 8, 18